Unto the End of the Earth

Richard D. Rigenhagen
with Carol Rigenhagen

Foreword by
John T. Maempa, General Editor

Kindle Direct Publishing

©2019, Richard D. Rigenhagen

All Scripture verses are taken from the
authorized King James Version.

Table Of Contents

Foreword

The Backstory

The Call

North to Alaska!
-We're Here! -First Flight -New Job -New Tastes

Wainwright
-Unforgettable Journey to Idaho –'Unto the End of the Earth' -Day-to-Day Challenges -Wings at Last! -Recovery From Re-covering -Back to Idaho -Disaster and Divine Delay -Deadly Encounter Buried! -Suzie -Dramatic Rescue -Challenges in the Arctic -Missionary and MAPS Connections -Slippery Slope! -God's Protecting Hand -Reaching Children and Youth -God-Ordained Visits -Crisis in the Air -Power of Intercession -Airplane Miracle -Emergency Rescue -Revival with Evangelist Warren Combs -Whaling Adventure -Family Visits

Shaktoolik
-Royal Rangers Adventures -Special Visitors -Search and Rescue -Berries and Bears -Ongoing Mission and Vision -Outreach Ministries -Search for a Hunting Party -Transition to Come -A Slow Journey Home

Fort Yukon
-Flying the Circuit -Engine Trouble -Blessed by CAP -Promise in the Sky -Arctic Circle 'Bump' -Sky Evangelism -Fort Yukon Pastorate -AIM Outreach -Airplane Trade -Rescue Mission -Troubling Encounter -A Disturbing Call -A Special Visit -Dwight's MedicalEmergency -Superintendent Tours -Overcoming Challenges of Change -Law Enforcement and Rescue Patrols -Ministry Transition -Expanded District Ministries

Emmonak
-Village Ministries -An "Old Friend" Returns -Draught of Fish -Snagged! -Mission Building Adventures -Crisis on the Ice -Caterpillar on the Ice -Search for Lost Boaters -Gathering Wood -Prevalence of Suicide -A Call Home for Christmas -Quick Return to Idaho -Tragic Death -Ice Jams and Fishing Season -Sectional Representation -A Generous Offer -Portland General Council -Mary's Visit –'Except a Corn of Wheat Fall' -More Shocking News! -Evangelist Warren Combs -Warfare Encounter -A Final Tour -Medical Challenges

Fort Hall, Idaho

-Spiritual Warfare -Jericho March -Amazing Transformation -Connecting with the Culture – 'Warriors for Christ' -A Super Invitation - Miraculous Provision -Invitations Abound -Heavy Anointing
-Invitation from TBN -On to Super Bowl XXX - Trinity Broadcasting Network -Memorable Moments -U.S. Missions Presentation -*Pentecostal Evangel* Interview -Winds of Change -ABATE Jack -Gathering of Many Nations -Growing Acceptance –"Stand in the Gap" Gathering - Attacks of the Enemy -Special Visitation - Warriors in Alaska

Motorcycle and Prison Chaplaincy
- Matter of Life and Death -God's Amazing Provision -Speed the Light Blessing -Hells Angels -A Vision of God's Provision -Vision Fulfilled - Trip to CMA National -Deer Encounter –"Law" and "Grace"
 -Carol's Amazing Resolve -Increasing Acceptance -Close Call -Crunch! -Riding Over the "Mighty Mac" -Pocatello Convention -Return to Idaho - Motorcycle Invasion –"Soul Zone" Is Born -Prison Invasion Partnership -Ministering in Maximum Security –"Mini-Sturgis" -Biker Sunday Gang War -Ongoing Ministry Outreaches and Events - Return to Michigan -Wonderful Reunion - Motorcycle Ministry Expanded -Back to Idaho - Health Crisis -Miraculous Recovery -Ministry Growth and Challenge -Looking Back as We Go Forward.

Foreward

Psalm 37:23 tells us that *"The steps of a good man [and woman] are ordered by the Lord."* When Rick and Carol Rigenhagen were united in holy matrimony on June 7, 1964, little did they know how their steps would be ordered a few years later. Rick was pursuing a good-paying job with Boise Cascade's sawmill in McCall, Idaho. Carol busied herself with being a homemaker and mother of their son Dwight.

Living in a beautiful log home nestled on a pine-covered hilltop, life seemed good. Yet, as both Rick and Carol grew and deepened in their relationship with God, something began to stir within their spirits. Unrealized initially by either of them, God birthed a special call that would take them, literally, from that quiet mountain community to the 'end of the earth.'

This expanded edition of *Unto the End of the Earth* chronicles many stories and testimonies of God's direction, care, healing power, anointing, and protection throughout their amazing journey of faith. Over the years, Assemblies of God U. S. Missionaries Rick and Carol Rigenhagen have been led by God's hand into unique, life-changing ministries that have dynamically touched Native Americans in Alaska and the Lower 48 as well as bikers and prisoners—ministries that continue in their retirement years.

--John Maempa
(Retired from 31 years of editing and publishing with Gospel Publishing House of the Assemblies of God, and nine years as Director of the Office of Prayer and Spiritual Care. John is also the sister of Carol Rigenhagen.)

The Backstory

I was born in Washington, Iowa, on August 2, 1944, to Art and Appy Rigenhagen. Dad was an accomplished mechanic and also owned an apple orchard. In 1946, Dad sold the orchard and we moved to Nampa, Idaho. We spent a few years in the Nampa-Star area where Dad was a mechanic. He later purchased a logging truck and began hauling logs for small logging companies. Then, around 1950, Dad purchased 80 acres of black pine timberland in Lake Fork and set up a private sawmill.

We began attending the Lake Fork Assembly of God church. God always came first in Dad and Mom's lives. I remember having family altar after evening meals. But for several years, I pulled away from God and began to go down a wrong path of sin and wild living. A praying father and mother kept me before the Lord during those years.

We had revival services during the winter of 1961, led by a Finnish evangelist. I went forward for salvation one night and the Lord not only saved me but filled me with the Holy Spirit as well. I laid on the church floor for four hours that night, praising God in a language that I didn't understand. I had no idea what was happening to me. However, I felt so clean inside that all I wanted to do was laugh and hug anyone I could find, asking forgiveness of all I had offended. I could not wait to get home and clean my room of books, magazines, and tobacco. I had a "sin burning" that night. My life turned around 180 degrees. I quit smoking, lying, and cheating, and attended church any time the doors were open. Did I ever fail? Yes, but I thank the Lord for His grace, mercy, and forgiveness.

Not long after my life-changing experience, I was voted in as president of "CA's," the Christ's Ambassadors youth group in the Assemblies of God. God moved on our group so powerfully. Some 25 to 30 youth attended our weekly services. I had never seen the Lord move so powerfully in all my life as He did those years. Services were held in the homes of various families, and many times the services lasted until midnight or later as the youth worshiped and prayed in the Spirit. Youth group members, Clifford Scheline, his brother Charles, John Maempa, and others received the spiritual foundation that would eventually lead them into full-time ministries. Many other people were called to be Sunday School teachers, and parents were inspired to raise their children with godly standards.

During this time, I proposed to Carol Maempa, the beautiful Christian girl I had dated for seven years. She is the second of three children of Ted and Mary Maempa who were farmers in the Lake Fork area. My brother-in-law, Reginald Gillatt, who had pastored the Lake Fork church, joined us in holy matrimony on June 7, 1964. For several years we lived in Carol's late grandparents' home located on the Maempa farm. Our only son, Dwight, was born two years after our marriage.

I worked for Ikola Logging and the Boise Cascade sawmill in McCall. During this time, I bought two new snowmobiles and began racing motorcycles. I also joined the McCall Flying Club, where I acquired my pilot's license and flew with the club for seven years. Little did I know then how much learning to fly in McCall's 5,000-foot elevation, snowy winters, and mountainous terrain would help me in years to come.

In 1970, my father built us a lovely new log home on a one-acre lot in a hilltop grove of pines two miles east of Lake Fork. Shortly afterward, Dad and Mom retired and moved to Star. With a good job at the Boise Cascade Corporation sawmill in McCall, life seemed really good, yet something was missing.

In early winter, 1972, God began moving me to dig deeper into the things of God. When we had revival services, I never missed a meeting. The Holy Spirit was preparing me for something, and I knew it; but I had no idea as to what was about to happen. During the time, Carol and I made a new and lasting commitment to each other and to the

Lord. The Word of God became very precious to us. I could not get enough of God's Holy Word. I asked for the precious move of the Holy Spirit in every service. Our pastors at this time were Louis and Nina Green.

The Call

On December 23, 1972, I went to work as usual, pulling night shift on the pond at the sawmill in McCall. The sawmill and pond were located on the southeast side of beautiful Payette Lake, a pristine lake with deep, clear, cold water. Winters in the mile-high valley were cold, with four to five feet of snow on the level, but the summers were wonderful.

Sturdy docks extended some 200 to 300 feet out into the mill pond. From there, I would jump onto the logs, carrying a 16-foot, lightweight aluminum "pike pole" to break up jammed logs. The pole had barbs on the end to stick into logs and pull them into a chute we called the "slip" or "bull chain." The logs were pulled up by the chain into the sawmill.

On that December night, it was just turning midnight when, suddenly, the Holy Spirit spoke to me in a way He had never spoken to me before. He spoke clearly, saying, *"My son, I have need of you in Alaska. Won't you sell what you have, take up your cross and follow Me?"*

Shocked by the unexpected message, I fell face-down on the dock and nearly went into the water! I began to weep and tell the Lord about all my failures and weaknesses, why He shouldn't call me, and why I wasn't worthy of such a calling. He reminded me that Moses said the same things when God called him. I continued my argument, pointing out that Carol said she would never leave Idaho, and that she would never marry a preacher. The Spirit said, *"I will take care of that."*

Then the Holy Spirit left me just as suddenly as He had come. I lay there in shock, pondering what had just happened to me. Then a shout from the sawmill jolted me back to reality; it was my boss. "How come the logs quit coming?" he demanded. I scrambled to get logs up the slip; but being so rattled by what had just happened to me, I sent red fir and spruce up with the pine!

I determined I would tell no one about what had just happened. I was in a spiritual daze for some time.

The next days were filled with strange and wonderful moves of the Holy Spirit in our home. I would ask Carol to pray over our food, and the Holy Spirit would fall on her. She would start weeping and crying out in the Spirit. "What is happening to me?" she would ask. "I can't even pray over the food without crying." I knew in my heart what the Lord was doing.

I prayed about and pondered what this calling would mean, how it would be fulfilled. How was God going to tell Carol? I knew that I would be flying a bush airplane in some of the most remote and dangerous places on the earth. I thought of the Lord's words, "Won't you take up your cross and follow Me?" I knew that God had asked the same of His disciples; several of whom died cruel deaths. Yet, I was resigned to the thought that maybe God was calling us to a mission where we would give our lives. But I had to know beyond a shadow of doubt that this was truly God and not just me.

About two weeks passed without hearing anything further from the Lord. Yet, Carol was still having extreme prayer encounters when the Holy Spirit would come upon her at strange times and places.

One evening, after I had returned from work and was relaxing in my easy chair, I noticed that Carol was staring at me with an almost angelic look. Then the Holy Spirit spoke to me and said, *"All right my son, she is ready; tell her what I told you."* I burst into tears and ran into Carol's arms, and with a quivering voice, told her that God had spoken to me about going to Alaska. She began to weep and cried out, "Praise God, it isn't Africa! I have known in the last weeks that God was preparing us for something really big, and all I could think of was that God was calling us to the jungles of Africa! But Alaska? Praise God! Let's get rid of this place and head north!" She was ready to go right then!

The Call Confirmed

A few weeks later, Pastor Lewis and Nina Green invited Carol and me to the parsonage for refreshments. While we were eating, Pastor Green asked, "Brother Rick, has God been speaking to you about something?" Shocked by his question, I just stared at him for a moment. He had a look on his face like Carol's when she stared at me from the kitchen a few weeks earlier. Not wanting to say too much at that point, I said, "Yes, the Lord has spoken to me, but I don't feel I should tell you what He has told us just yet."

"Well, be sure you take your snowmobiles when you go," he replied. "And Alaska needs missionary pilots."

Carol and I nearly choked on our food! We had said nothing to anyone about this yet. "God showed you our calling?" I asked.

"God awoke Nina and me and showed us your calling during the night of December 23," Pastor Green replied. He further shared that God had also told Winnie Scheline in our church and another brother. Now we had four witnesses to our calling without us having said a word to anyone!

That was all we needed. Immediately, I wrote letters to the Alaska District Superintendent, B.P. Wilson, and to Missionary Dale Umphrey in

Fairbanks. Pastor Green went directly to the Southern Idaho District office, over 100 miles away, and spoke to Superintendent Homer Walkup and the executive committee about our calling, and that God had confirmed it to him and Nina and others as well.

However, in the midst of these amazing events, not long afterward, I received an unexpected and devastating phone call. My fellow airplane pilot and dear friend, Clifford Figart, had been killed in a plane crash. I was very close to him, as he was a brother to my sister-in-law, Jan Maempa. Clifford and I shared a love for both airplanes and motorcycles. He was an airframe and power mechanic and worked at times on our club planes. He also was a wonderful Christian.

Hearing of Clifford's death, I was filled with fear and had doubts about our calling to Alaska. I never told anyone about my fears, but I was in an emotional daze until Clifford's funeral. He had a beautiful wife, Judy, and two small boys.

After the funeral, I sat with Carol at a table and tried to eat, but could only silently weep, feeling so fragile and unsure if we could answer our calling. Just then, Judy came over and sat down across from Carol and me. Though devastated by her loss, she looked into our eyes and lovingly said, "Rick, Carol, I know you are struggling with the call of God upon your lives because of Clifford's death. But Clifford would want you to look north with your head held high, and I do too. Answer the call with a strong, 'Yes, we will go'!"

I was shocked at Judy's inner strength at that moment in her life. We hugged, weeping.

Soon afterward, I received a call from Superintendent Walkup, giving Carol and me an invitation to go before the district presbytery during the upcoming meeting of the Southern Idaho District Council. When we went before the presbytery some weeks later, they questioned us in depth about our calling. At the end of the meeting we were enrolled in the Berean School of the Bible and given Christian Worker's credentials to get us on our way. We went back home to tell our parents and our home church about our calling.

Initially, Carol's mother, Mary, expressed strong concern about us selling everything and leaving. Her dad, Ted, however, more readily accepted it. My mother, Appy, also was terrified of us going off into the unknown. My dad, Art, responded much like Carol's dad. He pondered the calling in his heart and God made it known to him, as He soon did to all the immediate and extended family. They were assured that this truly was God's call upon our lives.

Around mid-May 1973, we tidied up our home and put it up for sale. After some negotiating on the selling price, in August we received an offer that was workable. It was hard giving up our dream home and launching out into the unknown by faith, but the call kept us looking north.

After paying off the balance of our home loan, we purchased a 1971 long-box Chevy pickup on which we mounted a new eight-foot, slide-in camper. To haul all our earthly belongings, my dad built a nice 12-foot, enclosed, insulated trailer with tandem wheels. We were ready to travel!

In the meantime, the Alaska District Council of the Assemblies of God had given us an invitation to come to Fairbanks to help Missionary Dale Umphrey finish building a native Assembly of God church there. Then the Southern Idaho District handed us our Christian Workers credentials and granted district appointment to Alaska to fulfill our calling. Several of our district churches invited us for services. I was shocked to get pledges of $150.00 a month. We paid off all our debts and had some $2,500 in cash for the trip to Alaska.

North to Alaska!

On August 24, 1973, we said our goodbyes, hugged necks, cried, and prayed together with family. Oh my! God came down!

We loaded our two new Polaris snowmobiles into the trailer along with all the possessions we could cram around them. I had not weighed our heavily loaded trailer before departing, but suspected we were loaded past safe gross weight. Amazingly, however, the trip, although slow, went quite well. Fuel consumption, of course, was terrible, around six or seven miles per gallon. We would go through a lot of fuel on the more than 3,000-mile trip to Fairbanks!

We headed north on Highway 95 through Bonners Ferry to the Canadian border, and stayed on 95 to Cranbrook, Canada. Then we took Highway 1 through Banff and Jasper National parks. What a beautiful trip! We saw bear, buffalo, mountain sheep, deer, elk, moose, and passed through more mountain tunnels than we had ever seen.

From there it was on to Prince George where we turned west and drove Highway 16 to Prince

Rupert. There we boarded our big rig onto a ferry named the "Taku." The fascinating three-day journey by ferry took us along the Alaska waterway and through the southeastern islands till we reached Wrangle, Alaska.

After disembarking, we left our rig in Wrangle and boarded a Beaver float plane and flew out to Zarambo Island, in the Alexander Archipelago of southeastern Alaska. There we visited Harold and Fay Fincher, long-time acquaintances and neighbors who had lived in Idaho. Harold was a logger, and he and Fay had moved out to the island to haul logs for a large logging company. There were only three ways to access the island—by float plane, boat, or helicopter.

During our five days with the Fincher's, we also ministered to the people in the logging camp. I also rode with Harold as he drove a huge logging truck and hauled logs to the beach and dumped them into the bay. Tug boats would "boom up" the logs and tow them to the Wrangle sawmill. Since the island gets some 260 inches of rain a year, it rained every day we were there.

Upon returning to Wrangle, we boarded the Taku again and continued till we ported at Haines, Alaska. We arrived in a driving rainstorm. After disembarking from the ferry, we had to go through customs again in order to go the last 300-plus miles to the Alaska border through the southwestern corner of the Yukon Territories of Canada. It was raining so hard it was scary to drive. To make matters worse, the heavily traveled, steep, twisting gravel road was filled with deep ruts and potholes, slowing our pace to about 20 miles per hour.

As we maneuvered this unbelievable road, the tandem axles on the trailer pounded up and down, and the springs on the truck bottomed out. Then it happened. The spring shackles on the trailer broke the bolt holding the axles in alignment, causing the rear axle to pull away from the trailer. Lying on my back in the mud, I jacked up the trailer as angry drivers splashed by. I found it hard to be positive, sweet spirited, and full of rejoicing at that moment. But, after much persevering, smashed fingers, and being covered in mud from head to toe, I finally got the trailer back together and off we went—but only 10 miles per hour now!

Finally, after two days, we reached the Alaska border. Upon clearing customs we drove our dirty, broken rig onto something I had never appreciated more—pavement! But even then, I couldn't drive very fast, as the frost heaves formed the road into a roller coaster.

"We're Here!"

As we pulled into Fairbanks at about 5:00 p.m., Carol, Dwight, and I looked at each other and began to weep. We hugged, prayed a prayer of thanksgiving, and found a phone to call Missionary Dale Umphrey. "We're here!" we cried.

Though we were elated to finally be in Alaska, it's hard to describe how we felt. Fairbanks was not quite what we imagined; it certainly had unique characteristics. The roads were paved for the most part, yet there were numerous dirt and mud roads or trails that came onto the paved roads from every direction. The trees were short, scrubby spruce trees mixed with birch, alder, and willow. Most of the trees had splits and pitch seams running up and down the trunks caused by the extremely cold, long winters where temperatures would drop to minus 50 or 60 degrees Fahrenheit for weeks at a time. This caused the trees to "cold crack" due to the moisture and sap freezing inside and expanding. Then when summer came, the trees would heal by sealing the splits with pitch. Though they might have been 100 years old or more, these trees that covered thousands of acres were only about 20 feet tall or less. Most of their energy was spent just trying to survive the extreme winters.

Welcoming us to Alaska, Dale Umphrey helped us find a nice basement apartment for $250 a month. It even included a garage for our truck. So, we settled in and found ourselves quite comfortable. We were shocked, however, at the cost of goods and services. Gasoline that had cost only 28 cents a gallon in Idaho, was now 50 cents a gallon. Food was the same way. We could figure on 50 to 80 percent higher prices at the stores.

Some wonderful folks from Graehl Assembly of

God church that Dale was building, had an acre or two about 12 miles north in a place named Fox. They allowed us to park our trailer and camper on their property, which was a blessing. Fox was a beautiful area that had been dredged for gold for some 100 years. The ground was very rocky with, thankfully, little mud!

I began assisting Dale with the church construction. Services were already being held in the basement which was mostly completed, but the upstairs was only just closed in.

A Native American brother named Howard had moved there from Iowa, following the call of God on his life as well. He was a large, strong man whom the Lord had delivered from a life of alcohol and drugs. Dale allowed Howard to live in a small missionary apartment in the basement. We all gave time daily to working on the church. Each weekday started at 8:00 a.m. with Bible reading, prayer, and coffee in the church basement kitchen.

Our long-bed pickup truck turned out to be a real blessing for hauling supplies, lumber, and other building materials. Dale was cementing rock into the foundation. We hauled the rock from the Fox dredge area. We would load the rock till the back of the pickup was nearly dragging the ground.

One of the rocks we found was particularly beautiful, but it weighed some 300 pounds. Howard and I wanted it very badly. However, not only was it heavy, it also was way down in the bottom of a dry ditch. Howard decided it wasn't worth the effort. The next morning, Howard was sick, so I said I would go get a load of rock.

"I'll bet you aren't man enough to get that big rock alone," Howard taunted as I was getting into the truck. What Howard didn't know about me is that when someone says, "Bet 'ya can't," I have a reputation for proving them wrong. I can still see Howard's eyes when I arrived at the church with that monster rock in the bed of the truck. I was going to get it even if it killed me, and it nearly did!

At first, Dale didn't want to put the big rock in the foundation as it was so much larger than all the others. But when he heard about how much blood, sweat, and tears went into getting it, he decided to include it. That rock was placed in September 1973!

Soon afterward, I went to Fairbanks airport to initiate an important phase of our ministry in Alaska. I signed up to fly two different airplanes to be used as needed. One was a Cessna 150 for when I needed only a two-place airplane; the other was a 172 Cessna Skyhawk that could carry three passengers. I got checked out by the rental company flight instructor and prepared to fly missions north, or to whatever destination would be required. I would continue to use the rental aircraft until we could raise the money for our own airplane.

First Flight

My first official missions flight was on October 23, 1973. Dale Umphrey, who served as a regional presbyter for the Alaska District at that time, asked me to fly him to the Beaver Village Assembly of God mission station. This would be about an hour and a half flight north following the course of the Yukon River.

The morning for departure was a clear and very cold, around minus 20 degrees. The flight base operator got the plane out of the warm hangar and readied it for use. Dale and I got in the plane and prepared to take off. It had snowed quite heavily before we left, but the snow was plowed off the runways. The runway was icy and slick; however, I had experienced similar conditions on many flights out of the McCall, Idaho, airport. So, this was already "old hat" for me.

Once we left Fairbanks, I noticed the lack of roads and large, flat fields that I could use for emergency landing strips in case we had a mechanical problem. I also spotted lakes and gravel bars along the streams and rivers that could be used if needed.

I had not been to Beaver village before, so I carefully followed the VOR (VHF omnidirectional radio range) and ADF (automatic direction finder) navigational aids that took us over the White Mountain range on the way to the Yukon valley where Beaver lay. Thankfully, the flight was uneventful, and the scenery was beautiful. The sky was so clear I could see the Alaska Range to the southwest and Mt. McKinley. When we landed at Beaver, the snow was deep, but the runway had been plowed nicely. However, it was frigid—minus 25 or colder!

Just a small Indian village, Beaver was home to only about 150 people. There was a small log church and log cabin parsonage. Everyone in Beaver heated with wood. There was no running water, so water was drawn from the river or melted from ice. Outhouses were used instead of indoor toilets. But, despite these minor inconveniences, what wonderful, friendly Christians were there!

While Dale took care of business, I sat with some of the believers who shared boiled coffee and Indian fried bread. After Dale's meeting, we prayed with the people. We couldn't stay long, as it was so cold the plane would soon freeze up without heat. We said our goodbyes and took off for Fairbanks. I was so happy that I wept and praised the Lord! Our missionary work had begun, and I loved it! I knew this was the first of many experiences to come.

New Job, New Tastes

Our money began to run low, so Carol and I took time to pray for the Lord to supply. The next day, I had a visit from the chief of security at the University of Alaska in Fairbanks. When he said he would like for me to consider becoming the first full-time safety and security officer at the university, I nearly fell out of my chair! "You will use a patrol vehicle to cruise the campus," he said. Then he added, "You could be a real blessing to these young people at the university. Can you start tomorrow?" So, for seven months, I was security officer. I really enjoyed the work, particularly since several native students also attended Graehl Assembly. These young people opened doors for us in the villages to the north.

One student named Hugo had recently been married. He and his wife were Eskimos from a village north of Fairbanks. One evening, when Hugo came to an evening meeting at the church, I noticed he was eating something that looked like chunks of watermelon out of a pint glass jar.

"It's pickled whale blubber," Hugo said, and he offered me some. Pastor Dale saw him offer it to me, and with a horrified look on his face, began to signal me with his hands and shook his head, "No!" But I remembered reading a book that said when building relationships with Eskimos, it helps to eat food that's offered, so I took a piece. Instead of getting just one, however, two pieces of blubber were stuck together.

"Eat them both, really good!" Hugo said. So, I popped them into my mouth.

The flavor was unbelievable! Later I would learn that the little chunks of blubber were raw and pickled in fermented seal oil. As vapors hit my nose, I wanted to spit out the pieces, but I remembered something else: "If you take the food, be sure you eat it and smile while doing it." So, I quickly chewed the blubber and tried to swallow it, but strong oil shot all through my mouth. I tried to smile, but it was more like a cringe. When I tried to swallow the blubber, it just came right back into my mouth. I swallowed at least five times!

By this time, Dale was rolling on the floor, laughing. My eyes were pouring out tears, but not from crying. Finally, I got the blubber down, only to have it come back to life in my stomach! It seemed to be sort of jumping around down there. I could tell exactly where it was at any time for the next few hours. I determined from that day that I would ask more questions about what I was about to eat. This would be the first of many food adventures to come as well.

Wainwright

As we spent more time with the Alaska natives in the far north, we discovered that they were very sensitive to spiritual things. We prayed with them often. We never had to wonder how they felt. They had faith to pray and to believe God for anything it seemed.

The next seven months flew by. I was flying on occasion and our son Dwight was busy in school. I was also working at the university, and in every spare moment I helped Pastor Dale finish the Graehl church. We both felt this was a learning curve for what was to come.

A powerful confirmation of what God was orchestrating soon came during a visit from the Alaska District Superintendent B. P. Wilson. He asked if Carol and I would consider being missionaries to the Eskimos in Wainwright village on the extreme north coast, some 350 miles above the Arctic Circle. Carol was ecstatic, but I was more reserved. Should we move out to a remote village 500 miles north of the closest road? I thought we would be flying to these villages from Fairbanks.

We decided to fly north by way of Wien Air

Alaska to Barrow, then take a small feeder airline to the village to see if we really could minister at Wainwright. So, on March 16, 1974, we flew to Point Barrow, the northernmost location of United States territory! We landed, making our approach over the ice of the Arctic Ocean. The temperature was minus 22 degrees; but with a 30-mile-per-hour wind coming off the ocean ice, the wind chill was around minus 70 to 80 degrees! From there we took a small feeder airline to Wainwright. When the pilot of the small 207 Cessna learned I was a pilot, he invited me to fly the fully loaded plane on the 50-mile journey.

Whenever a plane lands in Wainwright, it's a major event. It seemed that the whole village of 350 people was at the airport. There was much excitement among the Eskimo people, especially over the possibility that we would be coming to live with them.

After we greeted everyone, we were freezing cold. Peter, a deacon in the Assembly of God mission, took us on a wild ride through the village on a sled tied to an old Mercury snowmobile. Stopping at the church parsonage, we were surprised at how nicely kept the mission looked.

Peter took us inside the parsonage that was warmly heated with two stove oil pot heaters. There are no trees for firewood as Wainwright is some 200 miles north of the tree line.

Peter showed us through the home and the church, talked with us for a while, handed us the keys to the mission, hugged us, and left. We looked through the parsonage and discovered it had two bedrooms, a large kitchen and dining area, living room, a nice office with lots of shelves, large storage room, and a large fully enclosed porch.

We discovered there was no running water or sewer system due to the permafrost soil. Instead, there was a room with a 55-gallon barrel sitting on a two-foot-high stand with a water spigot on the bottom. Villagers, we learned, sign up at the store for water. The next day a track vehicle with a 500-gallon insulated tank delivered water for 10 cents a gallon.

Also, there was no bathroom as such; instead, the parsonage had a "honey bucket" room. The toilet inside was a painted plywood box with a toilet lid and seat attached by a hinge on top of the box. Inside the box was a five-gallon bucket. To reduce the odor, the toilet was vented by a three-inch flexible aluminum pipe that extended out the back of the box and went up through the roof to gently siphon off the odorous vapors. It worked amazingly well. When the honey bucket filled, it could be carried outside to the back of the house and poured into a 55-gallon drum. When the drum was full, the frozen waste would be loaded onto a sled and towed by snowmobile (or dog teams) to a dump about two miles east.

Situated next to the parsonage, the church was a 30- by 60-foot, two-story building with the main meeting area downstairs. Sunday School rooms were upstairs. Heat was provided by oil heaters on both levels. There was a small nursery also.

Dorothy and Allen Ahlalook, members of the church, invited us to their home for dinner that evening. Allen picked up us with his snowmobile. There were no roads in the village yet, so we went on trails to their home on the other side of the village.

Dorothy was the daughter of the previous missionary, Doris Fellows. Dorothy decided to make her home in the village with the native people. I really liked Allen who owned a dog team of some 12 dogs. The Ahlalook's home was very small but comfortable. Dorothy fed us well with southern, or "Lower 48," foods. We pounded her with questions. We had to know for certain that God was calling us to live and minister in Wainwright.

During our three days in the village, we visited all the people we could and also ministered in a Sunday morning and evening service. The services were awesome. In the evening service, we had a church full of people from the village. God came down and visited us with a powerful move of the Holy Spirit and a wonderful altar time. On Monday morning, church member Peter Tagarook took us to the airport on his snowmobile and sled. Strangely, at that point, neither Carol nor I were certain about ministering in Wainwright.

After boarding the plane, the pilot again invited me to take the controls. I taxied to the east end of the short 2,200-foot strip and took off into the wind; then I turned left and began climbing out toward Barrow. As I scanned the village below, I was suddenly overcome with tears and began to tremble. I felt as if I were leaving my home and family behind. I said to the Lord in my heart, *Yes, Lord, we will return to fulfill the call You have just given us.* A sweet peace filled my soul.

When we landed at Barrow, I told Carol what had happened to me as we were flying out of Wainwright. "You too?" she said. "That's what happened to me!" So, we visited the Alaska District office after landing in Fairbanks and told Superintendent Wilson of our decision to accept the mission at Wainwright. He was deeply pleased.

Unforgettable Journey to Idaho

Superintendent Wilson had suffered a stroke, and though he was recovering quite well, the stroke took a substantial toll. He decided to resign from his office and retire in Ephrata, Washington. Since he had spoken with Superintendent Homer Walkup in the Southern Idaho District about our taking the mission at Wainwright, we were invited by our home district to do a full district itinerary, and they would set up the schedule for us.

Learning that we would be itinerating in Idaho, Superintendent Wilson asked if we would help him haul their heavy items down the Alaska Highway to Ephrata in our four-wheel trailer. He offered to pay us for our efforts. I had no idea of what he was asking me at the time, but I said yes. So, we pulled our trailer to his home where his tools and other heavy items were loaded. Afterward, we placed our camper on the pickup and hooked the trailer onto the pickup.

I noticed the springs on the trailer were bent past straight, and the tires were half flat. So, I checked the tires and they were pumped to maximum pressure; but they still looked half flat. I learned that what Brother Wilson meant by "heavy stuff" were barrels of precious rocks that he had collected over the years in Alaska!

Not taking time to weigh the trailer, on March 30, 1974, we began our journey down the road, thinking that the Alcan Highway would be frozen and smooth. At least that was what everybody else had told me. What they didn't tell me about were all the 10 percent grades and mountain passes we would have to tackle on icy roads; not to mention that the Alaska Highway, at that time, was 1,200 miles of gravel!

Things went amazingly well until we hit the Rocky Mountains in the Yukon territories and encountered Pink Mountain pass. Entering the pass, we were forced off the grade by an eighteen-wheeler on a sharp corner. My trailer dropped off the grade on the right side and high-centered on the axle. I unhooked the trailer, and, thankfully, a large truck that came along hooked onto it with a chain and pulled it back onto the road. This, of course, resulted in a three-hour delay!

A few miles further, the road got very steep and the pickup began to spin out. So, I put on heavy duty chains which got us going again until we hit a 10 percent grade. By this time, it was dark. We got within 200 yards from the top and spun out even with full tire chains.

The temperature was well below zero, and the wind was blowing. Being dark and slick, I was concerned about trucks coming over the top of the mountain; I might not be able to see them before it was too late. I told Carol to hold the brakes on the rig until I could run to the top of the mountain with reflectors and flares to warn oncoming traffic that there was a problem ahead. I heard a big truck coming fast, and I hadn't placed the reflectors far enough up the road. When the driver saw our rig, he thought we were crossways in the road, so, to avoid us, he drove his truck off the grade into the deep snow, totally throwing off his load. No one was hurt, but that trucker was very unhappy!

Carol and Dwight went into the camper with the heat on and slept. I stayed up all night holding the brakes. Thankfully, there was little traffic through the night. Near daybreak, a large truck with tire chains came along and towed us to the top of the hill. We had to be towed at least four times during that trip. Even though the pickup had a 307 V8 motor and a stick shift, it could hardly pull itself in high gear on flat ground because our load was so heavy. When I came to any hill, I had to go to low gear. We could only average about 300 miles a day. Altogether, the trip took 10 days on the road. We were never so happy to finish a journey!

Leaving the trailer in Ephrata, we continued on our way. What a difference in power, performance, and gas mileage! We were getting only about six miles per gallon pulling the heavy trailer; now we were getting around 12 miles per gallon with just the camper.

Our itinerary in Idaho went well also. We had services nearly every night and picked up some $200 per month in pledged support which was a tremendous blessing.

With itineration finished, we headed north again for Alaska. We drove through Ephrata to pick up our now empty trailer and headed back up the Alaska Highway. This time we had little or no mechanical problems, and the trailer towed so easily. But, oh, that Highway! We had several flat tires due to the sharp rocks used on the road. Also, being summertime, the road was very rough and muddy in places. But, thank God, we safely arrived back in Fairbanks around June 25, 1974.

Upon arriving in Fairbanks, we began packing boxes to be mailed to Wainwright village as fast as we could. We felt a real urgency in our hearts to get there as soon as possible. We sent some 40 to 50 boxes; the largest were sent fourth-class mail. It took some three or four pickup loads to get the boxes to the post office. Then there was the $500 postage fee!

Graehl Assembly of God hosted us for our final service in Fairbanks and provided a generous offering. On July 3, 1974, we boarded a Wein jet for the one-hour flight to Barrow. Our son Dwight was only eight years old at the time, and for him all the traveling and flying was fun and games.

We landed at Barrow in clear, very cool weather. Summer temperatures that far north rarely rise above 45 to 50 degrees. We hurriedly changed to a twin-engine Otter plane that carried some twelve people and lots of freight. At that time of year, everything came to the village by air—food, snowmobiles, dogs, soft terrain vehicles, clothing, you name it.

After takeoff, we were amazed to see that the Arctic Ocean was mostly thawed, though there were icebergs. We also saw walrus, seals, bowhead whales, and numerous water fowl. There were geese of all colors as well as ducks and swans. On the land toward the south were thousands of caribou grazing and migrating. Small lakes dotted the land as far as the eye could see. There were no trees or willows, just grassy tundra and lakes.

'Unto the End of the Earth'

Upon our return to Wainwright, as we approached the village for landing, we saw people by the hundreds running toward the airport. When we exited the plane, there was a crowd of smiling, cute Eskimo faces looking at us. I overheard someone say, "There are our new missionaries!" Then another said, "There is their son, daughter, and Pastor, but where is his wife?" I laughed and grabbed Carol, who they thought was my daughter, and said, "This is my beautiful small wife." Everyone laughed and began hugging our necks. We surely felt welcomed. We were home!

A man with a Jeep pickup loaded our bags and drove us about a third of a mile to the parsonage that was situated only a hundred yards from the Arctic Ocean. Peter Tagarook gave us the keys to the mission and we went inside the parsonage. We were surprised to see that all of our boxes that we had mailed were stacked in the living room. The Wainwright post office was so small, that Peter, also the postmaster of the village, had them hauled over to the parsonage as they came in.

Things looked a lot different now as it was summer and no snow. But the water barrel was full of water. Little did we realize just how precious fresh water would be!

We counted our money and found that we had only $50 left. Thankfully, the church members had stocked our shelves with canned foods, flour, sugar, etc. Still, we needed some powdered milk, bread, oatmeal, boxed cereals, and other items. So, we walked to the village store. We had to ask where it was as there were no signs or paint on most buildings. The Eskimo children, intrigued by our presence, walked with us everywhere we went, showing us around. As of yet, we had no vehicle of any kind to use. We knew that God had asked us to live by faith, and that He would provide our needs as they arose.

At the store, we bought a few things and quickly discovered that everything was really expensive. Average cost of our supplies was 270 percent higher than in Idaho! After a long day, we went home, unpacked some boxes, and went to bed.

As we were preparing for bed, we noticed that all the blinds in the bedrooms were black and almost sealed off all the light from the outdoors. In the summer, 350 miles north of the Arctic Circle, there are 80 continuous days of sunlight! Now it was July 3, so the sun was still high in the sky at midnight.

On July 4, 1974, Carol, Dwight, and I had breakfast on the first day in our new place of ministry. It was a beautiful day; the sun was shining on the completely calm ocean. After breakfast, Bible reading, and prayer, I reflected on a statement

Carol had made while preparing breakfast. As she looked out over the beautiful Arctic Ocean, she said, "God called us to the end of the earth; if we go any farther north, we will be going south." I laughed, totally agreeing with her.

As we were completing our time of devotions, I asked Dwight to pull out a card from the little bread loaf-shaped Bible promises box we kept on the table. Before he read it, I said, "This will be our promise from the Lord for our entire work that God has called us to do from this day forward." I took the promise Dwight had pulled out and read it.

Go ye therefore, and teach all nations, baptizing them in the name of the Father, and of the Son, and of the Holy Ghost: teaching them to observe all things whatsoever I have commanded you: and, lo, I am with you always, **even unto the end of the world**. *Amen."* (Matthew 28:19, 20, emphasis added).

We nearly fell off our chairs. In light of what Carol just said about God calling us to the end of the earth, and now this Scripture verse drawn by Dwight at random. What an encouragement came to our hearts as God's calling was confirmed so powerfully through His Word!

Before that day was over, other things happened that further confirmed God's call upon our lives. Cathy, a young white mother of two little children came by to visit. She had been raised in Washington

State, but had met a native Eskimo man from Wainwright, fell in love, and married him. They then moved back to the village. Cathy had received some Christian teaching as a child but had walked away from it as a teenager. Now, she was struggling with separation from her family and friends and searching for truth and meaning in her life. We told her the story of Jesus and she accepted Christ as her Savior right there in the parsonage.

Later that evening, an Eskimo man named Steve knocked on our door and asked if I would come to his house to pray for his wife, the village health aid. She had fallen off the steps of their house and was sure she had broken her back. Wainwright had no resident physician or dentist, only Steve's wife whose medical training was somewhat less than that of a registered nurse. I followed Steve to his house, walking on the village "sidewalk" made from two, two-by-eight-inch planks nailed side-by-side on cross braces.

Entering Steve's home, I saw his wife lying on the floor on a mat, unable to move. I realized she needed a miracle. Kneeling beside her, I asked, "When I lay hands on you and pray, what is going to happen to you?" She smiled at me and said, "God is going to heal me!" As we prayed, she shook and cried. After the prayer, I told her, "Get up in the morning (which would be Sunday), and give your testimony of healing." I left their house and went home.

That Sunday was our first official service as new missionaries. I don't remember how many attended that morning, but the church was nearly full with parents and children who wanted to hear the new pastor. Cathy was there as well, full of the joy of the Lord.

During my message, the door opened and in walked the health aid I had prayed for! I stopped preaching and invited her to the front. With tears streaming down her face, she told her testimony of healing to the people in Eskimo language. The people began to weep and praise God in a loud voice. Then she walked out as straight and tall as she had come in. She was a Presbyterian and wanted to go over to her church for the service.

It took a while for me to settle things down and continue my sermon. When I asked what the health aid had said in her native language, the people replied, "She woke up with no pain in her back this morning!" This was the first of many miracles of God to follow.

Day-to-Day Challenges

We soon learned that just existing in the village required a lot of hard work. We had no washing machine or bathtub, so washing clothes, and ourselves, was quite a process. I would help Carol fill a 15-gallon tub positioned in the center of the kitchen floor. Dwight would take his bath, Carol next, then me—in the same water. Then we would add laundry detergent to the now cloudy water and wash the whites with a wash board. Carol and I would then wring out the soapy water by hand and lay them aside for rinsing later. Then we washed the colored clothes, wring them out and lay them aside for rinsing as well. After all that, I would finally dump out the water, which, by then, looked almost muddy. To do the "rinse cycle," we had to refill the tub with fresh water and go through the washing and rinsing process again. Our hands would get sore, dry, and cracked. Carol hung the clothes on wooden drying racks in the house in cold or stormy weather, and outside in the summer. Oh, how easily we take our modern conveniences for granted!

The kitchen sink and honey bucket room had drains that simply dropped the water under the house. The house was built on pilings sunk 20 feet into the permafrost soil. The house itself sat about three feet off the ground.

When we flew to Fairbanks for a minister's institute in January, we bought a new mini Hoover washer with a spin drier with some money we had saved up. What a blessing! We still had to fill it by hand, but it would pump out the water. The little washer did a great job.

In time, the villagers learned that I was a fairly accomplished mechanic, so I essentially became the village mechanic. Snowmobiles and ATVs were just starting to come into the village, and the native people didn't know how to work on them. So, I was able to make some extra money that way. Often, the people liked to stay and watch me work on their equipment which opened doors for further ministry. Many people were steeped in native religious beliefs. Oftentimes, I had opportunity to pray with them about various needs.

A native corporation soon also had me working on their large Terex tractors and trucks that were brought into the village by barge. These machines were used to help build roads in the village and upgrade the airport.

Overall, we were able to build wonderful relationships with most of the villagers. Peter Tagarook gave us an old Mercury snowmobile to use around the village. We already had a large wooden sled that was left by a previous missionary. Most of the villagers pulled their sleds with long ropes tied to their snowmobiles. That worked fine out on the tundra, however, a quick stop would cause the sled to ram into the back of the snowmobile. It also was tough to negotiate turns in the village with a sled on a long rope. I found that out the hard way one day. Going around a corner with a sled in tow, the sled swung wide and hit a frozen honey bucket barrel. The sled stopped dead, and so did my snowmobile. I kept going, however, through the windshield, breaking it into several pieces! I was badly bruised by the ordeal. I rebuilt the sled and put on a solid tow hitch.

Wings at Last!

As our ministry continued to grow, I felt an urgency to acquire an airplane as soon as possible. Two villages were without a Christian witness: Point Lay, about 100 miles west, and Atqasuk, about 60 miles southeast on the Meade River. Additionally, an Assemblies of God mission was to be built in Nuiqsut, about 250 miles east. Also, there was a great need to fly search and rescue missions from time to time. So, we began to pray in earnest that God would provide an airplane. Our first itineration in our home district would provide opportunity to present the need.

Sometime around mid-March 1975, Missionary Ken Andrus called telling me that he had an airplane for us—a Piper Tri-Pacer 150. Ken was one of the early Assemblies of God missionary pilots in Alaska. He asked that we come to Bethel where he and his wife Ethel launched the Far North Bible School for Alaska natives. He offered to fly his 206 Cessna to Wainwright and pick us up. All I had to do was help him re-cover the Tri-Pacer with Seconite, a Dacron-polyester material, and get it ready for our mission. Carol, Dwight, and I would then fly out to Idaho to raise support for the plane.

So, on March 28, 1975, Ken and Ethel flew to pick us up. Ken let me fly the Cessna most of the way to Bethel. The people of Wainwright were sad to see us go for a time, but they said they would continue to have services led by the church's deacons. They were such good people.

Ken and I went right to work on the plane. The Piper Tri-Pacer was equipped with Ferguson wing extensions. It was going to take a lot of work to rebuild the frame and cover the fuselage with the Seconite.

Recovery from Re-covering

Soon we had plane parts scattered all over an old military Quonset hut. We welded places in the airframe as needed, sanded the frame, and painted it with zinc chromate. After that, we pulled the Seconite fabric over the frame and began doping (gluing) the fabric to the frame. Then we used a heat lamp to shrink the fabric tightly onto the airframe like drum fabric.

At one point in the process, as I was using the heat lamp to shrink the fabric on the belly of the plane, there was a loud pop. The heat bulb exploded in my hand! Then, the glue on the fabric burst into flame. In a panic, I began beating the flames with my bare hand, but the fabric, made of synthetic fiber, melted into a burning liquid which resulted in third-degree burns on my hand. Yelling, I jumped out from under the plane. Ken, seeing the fire, dove under the plane and began beating the flames with his hand also. He too screamed as his hand was burned badly as well. Thankfully, Ken's son Brian had gloves on and was able to extinguish the fire.

Ken and I assessed the damage to our hands and determined right away that we needed to go to the emergency room. We both had burned our left hands badly. Skin was just hanging from our hands!

At the emergency room, a nurse bandaged our hands and sent us home. When we walked into Ken's house and Carol and Ethel saw our bandaged left hands, they thought we were pulling a prank; everyone in Bethel called us twins anyway. Thankfully, our hands healed miraculously fast. Everyone was praying for us.

Soon after we had the plane finished, we towed it out to the airport and installed the wings there. Ken's son Brian, a Federal Aviation Administration-certified airframe and power plant mechanic, assisted us and inspected all our work. After Brian did a final look at everything and signed the logbook, Ken got into the Tri-Pacer and taxied around a bit, then took off. He flew around for some 15 minutes and landed. Then I hopped into the pilot's seat with Ken along in the righthand seat. I was amazed at how well the old bird flew! I have to admit, however, that I wondered about all the bolts, nuts, screws, pins, cables, and safety wires, etc., that we had just taken off and replaced. I hoped we hadn't missed anything!

After landing, Ken climbed out and I flew solo for about an hour and a half to get used to all the plane's systems. It went well. So, the next day, Ken took Carol and Dwight in his Cessna, as I only had a "ferry" permit to take the Tri-Pacer into Anchorage for the final paint job and some mechanical work. I took off in the Tri-Pacer and flew through Rainy Pass to Anchorage. It took some four hours to make the flight as I had to land at McGrath to refuel. When I finally landed in Anchorage and taxied to the tower, I saw Ken and my family waving and smiling.

Back to Idaho

Upon securing my plane, all of us climbed into Ken and Ethel's Cessna and flew on to Fairbanks to get our pickup and camper for our trip, again, down the Alaska Highway. This time, however, there was no trailer to pull! What a wonderful difference that made on the trip. Instead of a 10-day drive, this one took only four easy, uneventful, almost boring days; and we used only half as much gas.

After arriving in Idaho, we immediately began our fund-raising itinerary and were amazed at the response. In one service in particular, in American Falls, God came down in an amazing way. A message in tongues and interpretation urged people to support our ministry. In response, people formed a line in the aisle and poured cash and checks onto the altar. The offering was over $2,700. In 1975 the dollar went a lot further than today!

I remembered seeing a plane in McCall that I had always admired--a 1951 Piper Pacer 135, that had been rebuilt by a machinist at the Boise Cascade sawmill. It looked brand new inside and out and was painted a beautiful cream color with a pretty green striping and interior. So, with the money that had been raised throughout our itineration, Carol and I decided to go ahead with the purchase. I called Ken Andrus in Bethel about our decision to buy the plane in McCall. We agreed to let him keep the Tri-Pacer and sell it.

We flew our new plane around McCall several times, taking friends, including our district superintendent, Homer Walkup and his office staff. They enjoyed flying over Treasure Valley and taking pictures.

Disaster and Divine Delay

After our final service at our home church in Lake Fork, a singing group that ministered in the service wanted to see our plane. When we got to the airport, the group leader asked me if I would take his wife and son up for a ride, but she was afraid of heights and didn't want to fly. But her husband insisted and literally picked her up and sat her in the front seat next to me. His son eagerly climbed into the back and buckled in.

All went well in through the taxi and takeoff, but as soon as the plane became airborne, the lady screamed and grabbed me around the neck! I was already too far into the air to land, so I tried to calm her down and gently started a left turn to go back for landing. But every time I moved the plane in any direction, she panicked. In all my flight training, I had never been taught what to do with a hysterical passenger! I kept talking and trying to get her to keep her hands to herself.

As I made a gradual descent over the Payette Lake to land, all went will until we flared for landing. There was some turbulence created by a 20-knot crosswind, and a gust of wind caught us just as I touched down, causing the plane to slide sideways. Then the left tire came off the rim and the rim dug into the pavement. That folded the left landing gear and the plane spun into a ground loop. Finally, everything came to a stop.

"Is everyone OK?" I asked. Thankfully, everyone was fine, but in the force of the wreck, the lady had bent the flap lever around my right leg, so I was caught. Fearing the plane might catch on fire, I said, "Get out quick!" So, we all jumped out. The lady's husband was running to us and as soon as he got to where we were, I said, "Wanna buy a plane cheap?" But he was not in a joking mood!

This whole incident was a difficult turn of events to understand. We were scheduled to leave for Alaska the next morning. Now, we had a badly damaged plane. *What now, Lord?* I asked. I was embarrassed and had more questions than answers.

Over the next few days, Carol and I spent much time in prayer trying to get a handle on just what had happened and why. Amazingly, a first-class airplane mechanic named Roger contacted me. He needed work and said, "Rick, I have just examined your plane. If you will allow me, I would like to dismantle it and haul it to the Homedale, Idaho, airfield where I have a shop. I can rebuild this plane better than it was, and you can help me. I will give you a very fair price." Then, much to my surprise, he added, "But if you open your mouth just once about Jesus, the plane goes out the door and I won't touch it again!"

After praying about this, I felt that God wanted me to accept his offer. My life would have to be the only Bible he would read. I let him know that he had a deal, so he hauled the plane to Homedale and we tore into it. After close examination of the engine, Roger noted that the crankshaft was bent, and there was terrible corrosion in the cylinder walls. "That engine wouldn't have made it to Alaska," he said. So, he totally rebuilt the engine and repaired the crushed airframe in the belly of the plane.

We sent one wing to Hubler Field in Middleton to get it straightened out and rebuilt. We also added Ferguson wing conversions which added 20 more inches of wingspan on each side, with beautiful droop tips. This feature would allow slower and much more controlled approaches to landing and permit shorter takeoffs. With less wing drag, I would also get about 10 to 15 more miles per hour when cruising. These would prove to be very good upgrades. Additionally, we installed the latest

Cleveland disc brakes, 700 x 6 tundra tires, and a Scott tail wheel to handle the uneven and soft Alaska terrain.

Throughout this process, Carol and I were so blessed by all the people that came alongside us with offerings and gifts. When everything was done, we had enough money to pay for the work.

Once the work was completed, I was almost afraid to get into the Pacer and fly it since the wreck, again wondering if we'd forgotten anything. But, when I took off, the plane flew like a new one! I was so excited to tell Roger how well it flew. After I told him, he said something completely unexpected.

"Rick, through all the skinned knuckles, extra expensive parts, and setbacks, you showed me something. Please tell me about your God!"

I was stunned but overjoyed to tell him the story of Jesus and our calling. While he didn't accept the Lord that day, and I don't know if he ever did, he surely was moved by all that had happened and by what I had shared with him.

We flew the plane back to McCall and packed for the trip to Alaska. Carol's parents wanted to trade their 1964 Jeep 4 X 4, three-quarter-ton pickup for our 1971 Chevy pickup that still looked really nice, so we did. They gave us some additional money, and we stored our camper and Jeep in their barn.

After saying our goodbyes once again, Carol, Dwight, and I climbed into our new plane on September 28, 1975, and took off on the 3,600-mile flight back to Wainwright.

We knew that winter was already setting in through the Yukon territories and northern Alaska, so we were very careful to check our pre-flight weather forecasts. We would be flying through the Rockies all the way to Alaska.

After clearing customs and overnighting in Penticton, Canada, we had breakfast at the airport. Then we fueled up and took off for Williams Lake, Canada. From there were went on to Prince George for lunch and more fuel. However, the weather from there to Dawson Creek was a concern. Strong winds would be blowing through the pass. But, if we didn't go at that time, a weather front moving in would ground us for days. So, we took off through the pass, and, boy, did we hit turbulence! It tossed our little plane around like a toy. Carol was praying, and Dwight was throwing up! I was sweating and trying to keep the airplane upright. Soon, however, the weather cleared and the rest of the way to Dawson Creek was great.

We overnighted at Dawson Creek, fueled up, at breakfast, and flew on to Fort Nelson. Though the weather through the pass to Fort Nelson was great, the temperature was getting colder. After lunch and fueling, I checked the weather to Watson Lake in the Yukon Territories. It would be cloudy with rough air, but flyable. So, we took off. The little Pacer handled the weather very well; I was pleasantly surprised. We landed at Watson lake and overnighted there. It had been a very full day and we were tuckered out!

The next morning was frosty cold. But, after refueling and breakfast, we took off for Whitehorse. I climbed the plane to over 10,000 feet as the mountains through there were very high. It made the ride smoother, but now it was really cold. At that altitude, the temperature was well below zero. But the heater in the plane worked very well, which was good since we would often be flying through sub-zero weather. We landed at Whitehorse and overnighted there.

The weather on to the Alaska border was a concern. However, again, if we did not leave, we would be stranded for several days. So, after fueling we took off for Dawson. We flew low through the pass over the Alaska Highway as it was overcast and had begun to rain heavily. I was concerned that if the temperature dropped only one or two degrees lower, we would have icing conditions. But, thank the Lord, that didn't happen. After passing Kluane Lake, we broke out into clear weather and landed at Dawson for fuel and lunch. Then it was on to Tok, Alaska, for customs and fuel. Even though we were very tired, we pushed on to Fairbanks and stayed overnight in the missionary apartment at First Assembly there.

On the next morning, I checked the weather up north on to Wainwright. Both Bettles, a small community with an airstrip, and the Brooks Range were socked in by bad weather. But, if we flew west to Kotzebue, fuel there, and then fly north over the De Long Mountains to Wainwright, the weather would be okay. Though it would make the trip about two and a half hours longer, we could get home that way. So, off we went. The rest of the trip was uneventful, and we landed in Wainwright just as it was getting dark. Praise the Lord, we had made it! With making so many jogs in our route it had taken 47 hours and 38 minutes to make the flight from McCall, Idaho, to Wainwright!

Wow! Was the village happy to see us! And they were so thankful for us to have the plane. It would prove to be a real blessing not only for ministry, but for medical evacuations as well as search and rescue. With this wonderful new tool for ministry, we were encouraged and ready to jump, by faith, into all that God had for us.

Deadly Encounter

One of our first mission flights was to Point Hope Village on the extreme northwest coast of Alaska. Peter Tagarook and his wife Bernice rode with us to see his brother, Greg Tagarook, who also was an Assemblies of God U. S. Missionary. As we flew toward Point Hope, we encountered low cloud cover through the De Long Mountains; however, the pass appeared to be clear through to Point Hope.

Yet, as we flew about half way through the pass, I was forced to fly lower and lower into the pass until we were just skimming over the river. By now the pass was so narrow that I could not turn around.

Then my heart jumped into my throat when I saw that dead ahead the fog went all the way to the ground! We were in a box that could kill us. However, I knew that the top of the cloud cover was only about 3,000 feet. I could see also that the pass was straight, and that the sides of the pass sloped pretty steeply. In order to climb above the cloud cover, I would have to keep the plane going straight on the current heading, climb as fast as the plane could climb, and avoid swinging to the right or left; otherwise we would hit the side of the pass. I shouted, "Pray!" and pushed the throttle to full power. Pulling hard on the controls, I kept my eyes glued on the artificial horizon, gyro compass, and airspeed indicator, not allowing the speed to fall below 80 miles per hour or let the gyro compass move one degree right or left.

That was the longest five minutes of my life! But soon we popped out on top of the clouds right at the 3,000-foot level, and we were dead center in the pass. "Praise the Lord!" we all shouted.

However, I could see that Point Hope was in the "soup," and there was not enough fuel to return to Wainwright. Additionally, the weather in the whole region was deteriorating. I turned southeast down the coast toward the village of Kivalina some 100 miles away.

By the time Kivalina came into view, a very strong crosswind of nearly 40 knots was coming off the Arctic Ocean. However, very low on fuel, I had to get down no matter what, so I made my approach to the runway. As I came in for landing, the wind was so strong that even by employing a full opposite rudder slip, I could not keep the plane lined up with the runway. So, pointing the nose of the plane into the crosswind, I "crabbed and slipped" the plane to touch down. But, to make matters even more challenging, the runway was covered with ice, and I knew I would not be able to hold the plane from sliding. So, when the plane began to slide, I crabbed the plane into the wind and let her slide, bleeding off the speed as quickly as possible.

After it seemed we had stopped, the wind actually kept sliding the plane sideways until it was off the edge of the runway and into soft snow. The sliding had been so gradual that when Carol and Bernice jumped out of the back door, they went up to their armpits in soft snow! By then a large crowd of Eskimos had gathered around the plane and they were laughing at the ladies stuck in the snow; then they happily pulled Carol and Bernice out.

I was concerned the strong wind was going to turn the plane over, so I asked the men to grab the wings and walk the plane up out of the snow and over to a tie-down, which went well. Thankfully, the plane was not damaged.

The Eskimos were such a jolly and kind people. One of the families invited us to their home for food and to stay the night. I was asked to pray over the food and I thanked God for a safe trip so far. Then Carol and I tried for, the first time, fish soup and Eskimo fried bread. It was great!

The storm blew all night, but the next morning was clear and cold. We went to the native store and bought seven, five-gallon cans of aviation fuel. With both tanks full of gas, we said our goodbyes and off we went to Point Lay. Thankfully, that flight was uneventful. Pastor Greg Tagarook and his wife were so glad to see us all. We had a great visit and spoke at their church and had an awesome service with them. We stayed overnight and left for Wainwright the next day.

Upon our return, the worst winter in 100 years hit the Arctic. Temperatures plunged to minus 50 degrees with 40- to 50-mile-per-hour winds that blew for five weeks. A lot of snow fell, which was blown into drifts 10 to 20 feet deep. It was so cold no planes could fly. The FAA ruled that small airlines had to stop flying when ground temperatures dropped to minus 35 degrees, as many airplane parts such as "O" rings, seals, hydraulic systems, and fuel pumps could fail in such frigid weather. Many days passed without mail or food supply flights. People with medical emergencies could not be flown out of the village.

Buried!

On one exceptional day in Wainwright, the temperature plunged to minus 58 degrees with a nearly 60-mile-per-hour wind, which drove the chill factor to minus 140 degrees! The wind blew constantly from the same northeast direction so that drifts formed great moats as deep and tall as the buildings. The sound of the wind screaming around those huge snow drifts was unforgettable.

Unknown to us, in the night, the wind changed direction. When we awoke the next morning, it was eerily quiet. We thought the wind had stopped. However, when I opened the door, a solid mass of snow filled the entire doorway! I checked the back door, same thing. I checked all the windows; snow was packed all around the house. We were imprisoned in our own house with no way to get out! I soon became very concerned. What if the house caught on fire?

I searched through the house looking for something to dig with. All of my shovels were in the shop twenty feet from the house. All I could find was a three-pound size coffee can. So, opening the door, I began attacking the hard snow with that can. Piling the snow in the porch, I dug a tunnel out a few feet from the house, then angled up till I broke out on top, about 10 feet up. I couldn't believe it! The wind was still screaming overhead. Since it was blowing from the other direction, all the moats formed by the drifts had filled in. I had to surround our tunnel opening with snow blocks like a fort and cover it with a canvas to keep the wind from filling in the tunnel. Finally, after one more day, the wind stopped, and the temperature rose to a "balmy" minus 35 degrees. I never thought I would consider that to be a warm temperature; but after what we had just gone through, it felt pretty good!

When I climbed out of our tunnel on top of the snow to look around, I was shocked. It looked like most of the village was gone. Nearly all the houses were buried under the snow. It was really strange to see only the stovepipes sticking out of the snow. Our parsonage had a flat roof, so the snow was blown level across the top. I could walk right onto the roof. I also could climb right off the snow banks onto the roof of our two-story church.

I noticed that there were very few people in sight. I walked over to the first person I saw. With panic in his voice, he said, "Everybody is trapped in their houses! We gotta dig them out!"

Everyone had an oil heater or coal stove, so we began checking on people by shouting down their stove pipes. It must have rattled some people when their stove started talking to them! We also banged on chimneys to get peoples' attention. We tried to find out who needed help the most, which was mostly the elderly. Though it was minus 35 degrees, I broke a sweat digging people out of their houses.

Eventually, we were able to dig out the big dozer tractors so operators could get started plowing out the airport. Our airplane also was buried under the snow. All went well, and more quickly than I thought it would. By the end of the day, airplanes with mail, food, and other supplies began landing. People that had been stuck in Barrow for many days came home. We were able now to fly people out who had medical emergencies. Since the villagers had snowmobiles, everyone got around over the drifts just fine. We never plowed the snow in the village; it was just too deep.

Suzie

During that incredible snowstorm we became acquainted with a lady named Suzie. Even though the entrance to our parsonage was only through a back or front tunnel, Suzie came over to visit us. She attended the Native Presbyterian church in the village, but she had become a dear friend.

We didn't even know Suzie was coming for a visit until we heard a woman hollering from the back tunnel, "Help! Help!" Since Carol, Dwight, and I were relatively petite, I hadn't thought about the problems a larger person might have getting through the tunnels. I opened the back door, and there was Suzie stuck tight in the tunnel! Carol went out the front tunnel to try help pull her out while I pushed and pulled from inside. We couldn't move her backwards, so Carol just pushed from behind while I pulled. I had to shave snow from the inside of the tunnel, but, finally, we got her in. Though she became pretty upset with me, I couldn't stop laughing. I tried to, but no matter how hard I tried to hold it back, I would burst out laughing again. So, I excused myself and went in the tunnel to make it bigger.

After finishing the job and regaining my composure, I went back in for coffee and Eskimo doughnuts with Suzie. All joking aside, during this visit, Suzie told us the most amazing story, one that we have shared with many people over the years.

Suzie had gone to the beach during the winter time to collect some coal. Wainwright was situated above a large coal bed about 30 feet deep. During heavy ocean storms, the waves would hit the beach and break loose chunks of coal. So, Suzie had taken some gunny sacks and a digging tool to work the frozen coal loose. However, there was not much coal where she first stopped, so being a fairly nice day, she decided to walk west down the beach to see if she could find coal elsewhere.

"I had walked maybe two miles and was busy filling my bags," Suzie said. "I decided I would come back later with my Ski-Doo and get them. What I did not notice was that a large polar bear was sneaking up on me. Suddenly, I turned and noticed that he was really close to me! I screamed and made lots of noise; I jumped up and down and acted really mean."

What made matters worse is that Suzie had forgotten her gun. She didn't even have a knife. And despite her efforts to scare off the bear, he just laid back his ears, reared up on his hind feet, and came for her.

"I prayed!" Suzie exclaimed. "When the bear grabbed for me, I threw my hands up at him and my right hand went into his mouth. I was knocked down hard on the ice, and I thought it was all over. *I am polar bear food*! I thought. But the bear turned and began acting very strangely. I just ran for all I was worth for the village. I knew that any second the bear would grab me from behind. But it never did; so I just kept running.

"Finally, I reached the village, frothing with sweat. I pointed behind me and hollered between gasps of breath, 'Polar bear! Polar bear!' Several Eskimo hunters jumped on their snowmobiles and took off back up my trail.

"After I calmed down and had tea with my family, I noticed I must have dropped my fur mitten from my left hand in all the excitement. So, I got my rifle and started my Ski-Doo and retraced my steps looking for my mitten. Then I saw the hunters standing around a dead bear. *Good, they got the bear*! I thought. When I pulled up and stopped, they asked me, 'Suzie! How did you kill this bear?' I told them that I didn't kill it, but that he nearly killed me!

"The hunters were very puzzled, 'This is how we found the bear laying here upside-down dead. No bullet hole, no knife wound, no blood anywhere. But look how the bear tore up the snow and sand all around here!' I asked them if they had picked up my fur mitten. They hadn't.

"As the hunters began skinning out the bear and cutting up the meat, they cut into the bear's neck. A hunter said, 'Look! There's Suzie's fur mitten stuck in the bear's throat!' Then everybody began to laugh; I did too as I realized how the Lord helped me kill that bear by choking on my mitten!"

Suzie was such an inspiration to so many. She passed on to be with the Lord. But, what a legacy she left!

Point Barrow Camp Meeting

In January 1976, we attended the Eskimo camp meeting at Point Barrow. Native people from all over Alaska flew into Barrow, even people from the Yukon Territories of Canada. I flew many people to that meeting from Wainwright. Though it was 25 degrees below zero, some 400 people attended. District Superintendent Willard Leisy was the keynote speaker. I also had opportunity to preach; many others spoke as well.

Oh, the Holy Spirit fell on that camp meeting! Evening services that began at 7:00 continued to 2:00 or 3:00 a.m. Great miracles of healing were witnessed, and many people received salvation; others were baptized in the Holy Spirit. During the singing and praise services, people were totally immersed in the presence of the Holy Spirit for hours. Some fell under the power of the Spirit and lay on the floor till the wee hours of the morning. God called people into ministry during those meetings, and many of them are in ministry today. Others have since passed into the Lord's presence.

Dramatic Rescue

Following the camp meeting, I was asked to search, by plane, for two missing men on amphibious ATVs. They had not returned to Wainwright from Point Barrow when expected. I took a spotter with me and flew along the inland trail; however, we couldn't spot them. We prayed for God's direction, and, as we flew along the coastline about 50 miles out of Barrow, we spotted them on the ice near the beach. I flew low and they signaled me to land on the ice to pick them up. However, I could see that the thick ice had broken away from the beach and new ice had formed.

From the air, the ice didn't look thick enough for a landing. But, the men on the ice tried to signal that it was thick enough, so I swooped down and made a fast, short landing. As the men ran to the plane, I noticed that the ice was bending under the weight of the plane. I screamed at the guys to hurry. As they started to get into the plane, I gunned the engine to begin my takeoff. The guys were still dangling out the door on top of each other; the situation couldn't have been worse. I had hoped to taxi back to where I had touched down, but that wasn't workable, and, now, I had less than 400 feet before hitting the water's edge.

The men added significant weight to our load, and with some two inches of crunchy snow on top of the ice, it took more power to gain speed. I feared we would go into the water before accelerating enough for liftoff. I cried out to the Lord and pulled full flaps at the edge of the ice and just skimmed over the water. What a relief as the plane began to lift! The men had managed to get all the way inside the plane and shut the door. We flew on back to Wainwright. Later the men were able to go back out on snowmobiles and sleds and retrieve their ATVs.

Challenges in the Arctic

By springtime, I had logged many hours of flying time in the dark, Arctic winter. Flying during the winter presented a number of challenges. If I waited till daybreak to take off, it would usually be dark when I returned. In the dead of winter, the days were very short. At 11:00 a.m. there would be only a predawn light; darkness would settle in by 3:00 p.m. Then, for some 83 days during the winter, we never saw the sun.

Electric power was very unreliable in the village as well. We were without power about 40 percent of the time. Therefore, it often happened that the runway lights would be off upon our return flights to the village. Sometimes I would buzz the village and several snowmobilers would speed to the airport and line the runway with their headlights. Or villagers would light six to eight coffee cans with gasoline in them to mark the runway. Many times, however, the wind would blow out the fires.

Missionary and MAPS Connections

On April 28, we took a long missionary journey to visit fellow missionaries in Kotzebue and St. Michael, then we went on to Bethel to take the plane in for its annual FAA inspection. Brian Andrus completed the inspection and performed the needed maintenance. We then took off for McGrath for fuel and a short visit with the missionary there. We then left for Anchorage. While there, our dear brother Ken Andrus had the radio shop install a new 720-channel King NAV/COM and ADF (automatic direction finder). Wow! What a blessing! This would give me a lot of confidence during bad weather and low visibility as I could always home in on the radio beacons throughout the state. This would be a real life saver. What a blessing the Andrus family was to us during our years in Alaska!

On the way home, we flew to Fairbanks, landing at Galena for fuel. But, again, the weather was bad across the Brooks Range, so we had to fly west to Kotzebue, refuel, and fly over the De Long Mountains to Wainwright.

As soon as we got home, we prepared to make an extended trip to Barrow to pick up Missionary Richard Potter and four MAPS (Mobilization and Placement Service) workers who were coming in on a Wein jet. Potter would be serving as missionary at a new mission in Nuiqsut village. Materials for the new mission had been transported by special permit to Prudhoe Bay on the oil field and haul road. There the entire materials package for the two-story mission would be loaded on a monstrous Rolligon cross-country flatbed vehicle. Oil companies used the Rolligon to haul supplies from Prudhoe Bay to the various test sites across the North Slope. Along with the building supplies would be a new Cushman Trackster.

My task was to fly Missionary Potter, the MAPS workers, and their tools and gear to Nuiqsut, some 150 miles east. Upon arriving in Barrow, Potter and two of the MAPS workers boarded the plane and we took off for Nuiqsut. I would return for the other two workers after the initial delivery.

Heavy fog settled into the area, and the clouds were low, but we prayed for God's help and were able to skim over the tundra, guided by the ADF and VOR radio signals. We landed just as the Rolligon was arriving in Nuiqsut with all the supplies. There were three helpers with the Rolligon, so, with the three of us and other Native brethren from the village, we unloaded the materials in a short time.

I flew back to Barrow to get the other MAPS workers and supplies. The days were getting longer, so I could fly many hours. Missionary J.W. Eaves, at the Barrow Assembly of God, kept fuel at the airport and used his 15-passenger van to bring supplies to me. After delivering the MAPS workers, I stayed at the village and slept on the floor at a Christian native family's home. They were all so sweet, and I got to try some new native foods. Much thanksgiving and praise, even during the mealtime prayers were offered for the new mission that was going up. That night, I was so tired that I slept like a baby!

Slippery Slope!

Securing a building's foundation in the Arctic follows the same process all across the North Slope. During the winter, a special drill rig bores down through the ice and frozen tundra to about 18 feet. For the Nuiqsut mission, 12 treated wood pilings were dropped into the drilled holes. We centered the pilings in the holes and poured mud around the edges, filling the holes to the top of the ground. The mud froze solid instantly and permanently. We then sawed off the pilings, leveling them at about three feet off the ground and proceeded to build the mission on top of them. During the summer, the ground thaws to only about three feet down, so the rest of the piling is frozen solid and does not move.

I could not believe how quickly the building went up. As I remember, we had the building closed in by the tenth day.

My last day there was especially memorable. We were roofing the building and it started to rain, so we all retreated under the roof for coffee and Eskimo doughnuts. After the rain stopped, we all went back up the ladder. I was first to get onto the roof. What I didn't realize at first was that the roof was now a sheet of ice! I fell down immediately and started sliding toward the edge of the roof. I was stories up, and the ground below was frozen—not a good situation! Thankfully, I had suggested earlier that we fasten a safety rope near the ladder. So, as I was sliding, I made a wild grab for the rope and got it just before going over the edge. I held on for dear life till the guys could pull me back up to the ladder hole in the roof. Wow! That scared me more than the many near crashes I had in a plane! I was thankful that we began every day with prayer for safety. God clearly was watching over me.

Harrowing Encounter at Home

That evening, I flew two of the MAPS workers back to Barrow then went on to Wainwright. When I got home, Carol was very upset. I could see that the porch entrance door was all chewed up around the lock. She tearfully told me that during the night a man began banging on the door to be let in. He sounded angry and intoxicated, so she didn't let him in. Then he got violent and began kicking the door and screaming at Carol. He found a tool on our porch and began digging and chipping around the lock. There were no phones in the village homes, so Carol had no way to call for help. Frightened that he was going to break in, Carol locked herself in the bathroom and prayed.

The man did break in, but he didn't find Carol. Angrily, he began tearing all the native artifacts off the walls, and then urinated on the floor. By that time, Carol, through her prayers, was filled with a boldness not her own. She came out of the bathroom, confronted the man, and said, "I believe it is time for you to leave—now!" The man just stared at her in disbelief as if he had just seen an angel. He stumbled around, grabbed his things, and ran out. Sadly, the man got on an ATV and ran into the back of a truck and was killed. Though we did not understand that kind of ending for him, the Word of the Lord declares, "Touch not mine anointed, and do my prophets no harm" (1 Chronicles 16:22, KJV). This man had many chances to walk with God, but the way of the transgressor is hard.

God's Protecting Hand

Later, I received a message that I was to call Superintendent Willard Leisy on the village phone in the city office. He would be flying into Barrow on a Wein jet the next day and asked if I could fly up to meet him there, then go back to Nuiqsut and spend a week with him working on the mission. It would be a tremendous honor work alongside Superintendent Leisy for a week, so I flew to

Barrow the next morning.

Upon checking weather conditions at the flight service center, I learned that the Colville River had broken up and there was a big ice jam down river that caused the water to back up and flood the Nuiqsut airstrip. Yet, the report indicated that the water had subsided overnight, so I should be able to land. However, when we flew over the airstrip, Missionary Richard Potter was waving a white flag indicating, "Do not land!" I could see why; there was a thick skim of mud about two or three inches deep all over the runway. So, I made a flying "touch" to test the firmness of the airstrip. Poor Richard was in a frenzy by this time! But I landed slowly, with a full stall landing yoke in my lap which kept the plane from going over on its nose. Mud flew everywhere, but nothing was damaged. Richard was in a sweaty lather, but we all had a good laugh when it was over. Since we would be there for five days, the strip would be dry enough for takeoff by that time.

Richard had loaded all our gear, tools, sleeping bags, and supplies into his Speed-the-Light Cushman amphibious trickster and took us up the hill to the gleaming new Assembly of God mission. By this time, the building project was getting well along. The wiring was all in, so we went to work insulating and hanging sheet rock on the walls.

We camped inside the building and did most of our cooking on a Coleman pump gas stove. The weather was getting very spring-like with lots of sunshine along with heavy fog at times. Richard was very excited about their new mission. We spent a lot of time holding evening services and in joining together in prayer. Overall, the work was going very well, and soon it was time to return home.

Saturday morning's weather was a bit questionable, but I went on down to the airplane to check out the runway condition and go over the plane. I checked all the things that a pilot normally reviews before a flight. As I did so, I noticed that an inspection cover on one of the wings was reversed and appeared to have been tampered with. So, I removed it and looked inside. To my horror, someone had removed all the control cable safety wires and had loosened the turnbuckle cranks. Seeing this launched a fine-toothed examination of the whole plane. The tampering that had been done could well have caused a fatal crash. Though I reported this to the authorities, to my knowledge, no one was ever arrested for it.

As Superintendent Leisy and I prepared to take off for home, I could see that the mud on the runway was still quite soft, so I put a one-by-eight-inch, 16-foot board under the tail wheel to give me a little head start on our takeoff run.

Since we were heavily loaded, the tail wheel really dug into the mud, causing a lot of drag. So, I shoved the yoke all the way forward and gave full power to the engine with flaps and the plane accelerated nicely and rose quickly.

As we got about halfway to Barrow, the cloud cover began to force us lower and lower. Soon we were down to minimum level for safe flight. I radioed Barrow for weather updates and they informed me that the weather at Nuiqsut had just dropped to zero with ice fog. Barrow was now operating under special visual flight rules (VFR)—a set of guidelines pilots operate under when conditions still allow the pilot to see the terrain. However, due to severe icing conditions, Barrow would go to IFR or instrument flight rules within one hour. My heart leaped to my throat. We could not go back, and we were still 50 minutes out of Barrow; to make matters worse, we were already picking up ice on the plane.

In a few minutes, the fog went all the way to the ground and we were icing badly. I radioed an emergency to Barrow, but they did not hear me. No one would hear us now—except the Lord! Brother Leisey and I began to pray. An emergency landing right then definitely would not go well.

Five pastors had flown into Barrow for the meeting. Sensing our crisis, Pastor J. W. Eaves told them, "Brothers pray! Rick is in trouble in the plane!" So those five men of God went to their knees and touched heaven for us.

As I was setting up an emergency landing on the rough tundra, what appeared like a tunnel opened up toward Barrow. The fog lifted up right in front of the plane just enough for us to fly in clear weather! But, 100 yards on each side of the plane was solid ice fog. I kept trying to contact Barrow, as I could hear them calling me, but they could not hear my transmissions.

We flew on, skimming over the tundra for some 30 minutes. I stayed right in the center of the "tunnel" as it was pointed straight for Barrow. Then, the bright orange natural gas line that supplies Barrow came into sight. I was so excited as I knew the pipeline went straight to the east end of the airport. I grabbed the mike and shouted on the radio. "Barrow Radio, this is Piper 2698A, I have the pipeline east in view; we are coming home!" The controller, nearly shouting over the radio, said "98A, we thought you had gone down in the ice fog. We clear you into the Barrow control area, special VFR. But hurry, the fog is dropping fast!" Yes, it was dropping; we could se it. Then I saw the end of the runway and touched down onto the strip just as the fog totally closed in. Praise the Lord again for His protection!

Reaching Children and Youth

As our ministry in Wainwright progressed, Carol and I felt that we really needed to do something special to get to the hearts of the children and youth in our village. So, Carol began a Boys' and Girls' Bible Club, and I started a Christ's Ambassadors youth group. Carol got a top-of-the-line "Show and

Tell" projector to assist her in telling Bible stories. For the youth group, I built a ping pong table and purchased a new 16-millimeter movie projector. This was very new technology for the villagers as television had not yet come to the village; it really drew youth to our services and meetings.

We acquired movies such as *Thief in the Night* and *Distant Thunder.* Eventually, we secured a whole series of movies relating to the end times. How the Lord poured out His Spirit on the youth and children during that time! Many of them found Jesus as their Savior and experienced the baptism in the Holy Spirit. There was such a hunger for more of God in their lives. Every day after school, ten to twelve children and youth would run to the parsonage and bang on the door. They would say, "Pastor, can we come in and pray in the living room?" How could I say no to a request like that! In my heart I still can hear those kids crying out to the Lord. Many times they would end up lying on the carpet totally lost in the Holy Spirit. In church services, the children would sit on the front pews anticipating the move of the Holy Spirit.

I will never forget one stormy Sunday night when the village power went off as it often did. We had an emergency light plant, but the Presbyterian church didn't. So, during power outages, our church would often overflow with people.

I was beginning my sermon when one of the youth on the front bench began to tremble and weep in the Spirit which spread across the bench until all the youth were in the Spirit with their hands raised toward heaven. Then, like a wave, the Spirit of the Lord began to move among the adults all the way back to the Presbyterian visitors. At that point, I just released the service to the Holy Spirit. I knew He could do more in a few moments than I could do in a lifetime. And He did!

Flowing with the Spirit

We saw great healings during those days. During one service, Anna, a usually quiet, soft-spoken lady, came running toward the podium. I asked, "Anna, what do you need from the Lord tonight?" She said, "Pastor, you and these people know about my paralyzed arm. I can hardly move it and it hurts most of the time. Tomorrow, I am supposed to fly to Barrow and a doctor is going to attempt to attach the damaged nerves so I can use my arm again. But, tonight, I believe God is going to heal me! Pastor will you please anoint me with oil and pray the prayer of faith?"

As I prayed, Anna took off running back and forth in front of the altar. Then, with her paralyzed arm, she grabbed a huge Bible from the Communion table and raised it above her head and began waving it around praising God, dancing in the Spirit! At that point, the church erupted in praise to the Lord! I don't remember how long that service lasted, but no one cared.

I learned early on that when the Holy Spirit moved, it didn't matter what part of the service we were in, I knew we needed to get out of the way, let go, and let God have His way. Some will criticize this saying, "But that is just emotionalism." Really? What about the fruit? The fruit of those days in Wainwright is still there today. It would be an amazing experience to see what really happened on the Day of Pentecost, the Great Awakenings of the early 1700s and 1800s, the Azusa Street Revival with William J. Seymour, and the Welsh Revival of the early 20th century. I am ready for it again! Regrettably, man's interventions, thoughts, philosophies, and ideas of what should be have dispelled great revivals.

God-Ordained Visits

Carol and I flew to Anchorage for District Council at the First Assembly of God church. I was greatly surprised to see Reverend Burl Duncan from Idaho there. When I asked what brought him to Alaska, his response was, "I don't have any idea. God just spoke to my heart to go to Alaska District Council. So, I packed my suitcase, bought a ticket, and here I am." Immediately, I realized that God had brought him to preach revival services at Wainwright. Carol and I had been praying for a follow-up revival to what God had been doing there.

"Would you fly back to Wainwright with us in our little plane to have a revival with us?" I asked. His response, with tears, was, "Praise God, yes!"

The native people dearly loved Brother Duncan. He brought a message of spiritual strength to our people, focusing on the key doctrines of salvation, divine healing, and the baptism in the Holy Spirit. Yet, I knew there was another purpose in his coming. He would take a message of need back to the Southern Idaho District.

While Brother Duncan was with us, it was very cold and windy. When the wind would come off the ice pack at 30 to 40 miles per hour, the linoleum in our kitchen would float up off the floor about three to four inches, making the floor very cold. Brother Duncan puzzled over how that could be remedied as the parsonage was built up about three feet off the ground to keep the permafrost from melting under the house. We concluded that we needed foam-backed carpet tile that would be glued down. But, there was no money for that. In fact, due to finances, we were running low on food. We were praying in every bit of food and ate lots of caribou, fish, and instant potatoes.

Near the end of his visit, we sat down with Brother Duncan for breakfast with only one egg and a little toast between us. We prayed over the food, but Brother Duncan couldn't eat; he just wept and prayed some more. While we were eating, there was a knock at the door, and there stood Sister Amy Patkotak with two large bags of store-bought food! She said, "God woke me last night and told me to buy you folks some white man foods this morning. I am so happy in my soul to be a blessing to you now that I see your situation. Praise God!" We all began to worship and praise the Lord for His great provision again.

Amazingly, there was a good enough offering taken at church for Brother Duncan to get a plane ticket from Wainwright back to Anchorage. At that time, he could fly back to Anchorage less expensively on a commercial plane than what it would have cost me to fly him there.

As soon as Brother Burl's feet hit the Idaho tarmac, he went to work having services, writing letters, and making phone calls. Soon two large boxes of foam-backed carpet tile arrived. Carol and I went right to work ripping out the old linoleum. Then we cleaned and painted the floor to make the carpet tiles adhere really well. Wow! What a difference that made. And the tiles were a beautiful shade of green. Now the floors were barefoot warm all winter!

In addition to the tiles, weekly boxes of fruit, vegetables, and down-home foods of all kinds began arriving from women's ministries groups in Southern Idaho. We were so thankful for Brother Duncan's efforts to encourage groups to partner with us.

Later that summer, another great man of God came our way—Charley Hudspeth. He came for two weeks of services. Also, during that time, Reverend Greg Tagarook and his wife Dorcas flew up from Point Hope which is located way up north on the west coast, not far from Siberia. What a move of God we had during those meetings!

Brother Charley was a songwriter as well. He had written a song for the far north Eskimos, in which the chorus went, *"Believe, receive, that's all you have to do. Reach out, don't doubt, just let the Lord bless you!"*

On Saturday evening, Brother Greg and Dorcas wanted to get back to Point Hope for the Sunday morning service. So, I fueled the Piper and boarded Brother Greg, Dorcas, and Charley along with lots of luggage and taxied to the end of the runway. Wind and temperature were favorable, so, after a prayer, I fire-walled the throttle. Using all of the 2,200-foot runway, the little plane climbed out quite well, despite the heavy load and low-powered engine. We climbed to 4,000 feet and headed to Point Hope some 240 miles southwest. It was a beautiful, two-hour flight down the Arctic coast. We saw hundreds of seals on the ice floes and thousands of birds.

Point Hope is on a sand-gravel spit several miles out in the Arctic Ocean from the mainland. Whale bones are stuck in the sand around the airport and the village, a testament to the many bowhead whales that the people had hunted successfully over the years.

Upon landing, we caught a ride to the village with some folks on an ATV pulling a trailer. We refreshed ourselves and had dinner with Pastor Greg and Dorcas. Afterward, Greg helped us get four cans of airplane fuel from the native store. I always carried a chamois-skin-covered tractor gas funnel to filter the fuel while filling the tanks as oftentimes there would be rust and sometimes moisture in the sealed cans due to condensation. Charley took lots of pictures, then we said our goodbyes and took off back for Wainwright.

Nearly halfway to Wainwright, Charley realized that he had left his pulpit Bible at Greg's church and nearly panicked. "We have to go back and get it!" he said. That would mean getting the store manager out of bed as well as getting a ride back to the village. I assured Charley that he could use one of my Bibles and that I would call Greg to put the Bible on the next plane to Wainwright. Charley was okay with that. And, by the way, he preached just fine from my Bible! His was returned to him in a couple of days.

During this time, the Alaska North Slope Department of Public Safety was gearing up to come to Wainwright to build a public safety building and small jail. They also would supply a couple of officers. Since I had the only plane for a hundred miles, I was called upon to fly numerous missions for them, including search and rescue and medical evacuations to Point Barrow hospital. One of the officers became a vibrant Christian, attended church, and could play a trumpet and accordion at the same time. This was awesome to watch and hear! He played just the bass keys on the accordion with his right hand and the trumpet with his left. He was a one-man band for the Lord!

That winter, I was having trouble with ice crystals forming in the airplane fuel. When the temperatures dropped to minus 30 or 40, the crystals would actually shut down the engine in flight! It would tend to be a bit unsettling to passengers when I had to dive for an ice floe, beach, or frozen lake to make an emergency landing. Thankfully, I never wrecked a plane in all my flying in Alaska.

Though the FAA does not recommend flying at such low temperatures, they do approve mixing one percent denatured alcohol with the fuel to eliminate the ice problem, and it doesn't hurt the engine. So, I always added an eight-ounce bottle to each fuel tank before takeoff. I also plated up the air-cooling vents in front of the engine cowl, as the engine would run too cold in those temperatures. Plating the front of the plane kept the oil temperatures around 180 degrees.

Crisis in the Air

We sure loved our little Piper PA-20, but it was underpowered for the things I needed it to do. However, I could land the Piper in places that normally would be hard to get out of as the small plane could take off on a shorter than usual runway. At one point, I had opportunity to fly a PA-20 with a much more powerful engine and a performance prop. Wow! What a difference! I knew I had to get my plane converted soon.

After two years of flying the PA-20, we were invited to Idaho again for several services to raise money to get the new engine. So, before we left, we arranged to have two native intern pastors stay at our Wainwright mission to cover for us till we returned.

On May 7, 1977, we took off for Idaho in our little plane. The weather was bad over the Brooks Range, so, again, we had to fly west to Kotzebue for fuel. After landing at Kotzebue, I checked the engine and noticed it was two quarts low on motor oil. This was unusual as it had never used oil before. So, I did a thorough check of compression and checked for leaks; all seemed fine. However, the weather to Fairbanks was questionable. When I asked about the next day's weather, I was told that a bad front was moving in from the west and that we could be stuck at Kotzebue for several days.

Against my better judgment, I decided to take off for Fairbanks even though it would be dark in an hour. I didn't mind night flying, but flying in questionable weather over mountains with a single-engine airplane was another matter. We were just anxious to get out of town. We took off and all went well for the first hour, then it got dark—really dark. Neither the moon nor stars were visible. We were flying over a very remote area with little or no civilization, so not even ground lights could be seen.

About 45 minutes into our night portion, I noticed the engine didn't sound right. So, I did a thorough engine instrument scan. To my great concern, the oil pressure needle was low into the red and getting lower, and the engine temperature was moving rapidly into the red line! I immediately woke Carol who was asleep in the back seat. I said, "Carol, pray. The engine is going to seize in a few moments!"

I turned on the landing lights only to see that we had entered a blinding blizzard! Conditions couldn't have been worse. The landing lights made everything crazy so I turned them off. I pulled the power back to about fifty percent and went to a full rich fuel mixture to cool the combustion. Amazingly, at that moment I felt a wonderful, warm presence in our plane, so much so that I began to weep. I did another instrument scan and saw that the oil pressure was beginning to rise. It slowly rose into the high yellow, and the engine temperature came down also into the high yellow. I cried out to the Lord. "Dear Jesus, all we need is 20 more minutes to make Fairbanks"! Carol was lost in the Holy Spirit as she interceded in the back seat.

For the moment, we maintained altitude. Below us

was almost certain death if we had to crash land in the mountains. I contacted Fairbanks air traffic control and declared a "pan-pan," a communication that signified a state of urgency on board. This was less urgent than a "mayday" call which would signal imminent danger to life or the function of the aircraft. I was not yet ready to send that message.

Traffic control gave me a transponder "squawk" code and then said, "2698A we have you 60 miles west and will call every minute for status update of your flight."

"Please, just 20 minutes Lord!" I prayed again. The next minutes were almost uneventful except for the calls from traffic control. Then, suddenly, we broke out of the clouds and straight ahead was a beautiful sight—the city of Fairbanks in all its glory and bright lights. The runway lights were on high intensity. Carol and I broke into praise and thanksgiving to the Lord. I told control, "Fairbanks in sight and I still have 4,000 feet; request straight-in approach".

"Any runway is yours" control replied. "The area is clear of all aircraft."

To save what was left of the engine, I pulled the power off and did a dead-stick landing. Once we were safe on the ground, I didn't care if the engine blew, so I gave it a shot of power to taxi to the tie-down area. It was running, but not well. Upon shutdown and initial inspection, I saw that the whole plane was bathed in oil that had spewed from the crankcase breather. Engine tear-down later indicated that a piston had broken around the head and the ring lands or grooves were broken allowing the combustion to go by the piston into the crankcase. This pressurized the crankcase, blowing the motor oil out of the breather. But we were alive and safe to the glory of God!

This meant that we would have to fly commercial from Fairbanks to Idaho and leave our Piper in Fairbanks until we returned with the money for a new engine. Pastor Edward Hughes of Fairbanks First Assembly of God invited us to stay at their missionary apartment with a courtesy car included. He also invited me to speak at their church on Sunday. God gave us a powerful service that day, and an offering of over $1,600. Pastor Hughes said to me, "Brother Rick, don't just get a new engine for your old plane, get a new plane." Wow, that was going to take faith!

When we got our tickets to Boise, Idaho, we were surprised to learn that we were going to fly on a 747. That monster had 10 seats across and two separate aisles. I could have nearly landed my Piper on one of the wings! As the monstrous jet filled with people, plus cartloads of baggage, and some 40,000 gallons of fuel, I wondered how there could be enough runway for it to take off. But when the moment of takeoff came, no problem! The pilot didn't even use all the runway. What an experience!

When we arrived in Boise, my in-laws, Ted and Mary Maenpa, were there to meet us. We were going to need transportation for itineration, so we went to a Chevrolet dealership and bought a two-year-old, three-quarter-ton, long-box pickup to haul our camper we had stored in my in-laws' barn.

Our itinerary this time took us across the country. Leaving Idaho, we drove all the way to Springfield, Missouri, where we visited Carol's brother John Maempa and his wife Jan and two children. We had services in Springfield while there. Then, heading back west, we went to Colorado and had services scheduled with the Lewis Green family, then to Devils Lake, North Dakota, where we had services with Pastor Clifford Scheline. From there we returned to our home district in Idaho. Funds had come together well for a new plane; we had already received around $9,000 toward it.

Power of Intercession

During a service at First Assembly of God in Idaho Falls, an elderly lady came up to me and shared something we will never forget. She asked, "Were you and your family in trouble in your plane on May 8th around 2:00 a.m.? After mentally calculating the differential between Alaska time and Idaho time, I realized that she had identified the exact time we were in crisis.

She went on to say, "I was fast asleep when, suddenly, the Lord woke me, giving me a vision of you and your family in a small plane flying in a storm. I saw the plane going down and crashing into a rock mountain in a fire ball! I immediately dropped to my knees by my bed with a crushing burden in my soul for you. Then, the burden suddenly lifted and I crawled back into bed in sweet peace."

When I asked the dear sister how long she had prayed, she recalled that it was around 20 minutes. Wow, 20 minutes! That was the time I had asked the Lord for to make the landing in Fairbanks that night! Clearly, it was not our time to enter eternity yet.

Airplane Miracle

Our next services were at First Assembly and Faith Assembly in Twin Falls. Since we arrived on Saturday, we drove out to the airport. I had heard about a like-new Maule Strata Rocket 210 airplane for sale and wanted to see it. I immediately fell in love with the plane and called the owner. He came over and I got to fly it. What a powerful, wonderful plane. He wanted $19,000 for it, which was a fair price; but, he made it clear that he had no love for God and that he didn't care that I was a missionary for Jesus Christ. I asked if he would take $9,000 with the understanding that I would raise the rest in 30 days.

"I will do that on only one condition," he said, "that it be on a win-or-lose-all-in-30 days contract."

"No way!" I said. I had never gambled, and wasn't about to start then, especially with God's money. I assumed that I would not see that plane again.

That night was one of the most troubling nights of my life. The Lord began to speak to me in the night. *"What is real faith to you my son?"* He asked. *"Is it leaving a way out? Do you have faith for that airplane or not? When I called you, did I not call you to a life of living by faith?"*

I tossed and turned through the night. By morning, my heart had changed. I went back to the owner of the plane and said, "Here is $9,000 of God's money. If I do not lay the remaining amount in your hands in 30 days, the $9,000 is yours to keep. And if that happens, I will walk out of here with my head held high believing with all my heart that I had done exactly what God told me to do!" I pretty much stood alone in that decision, except for my sweet wife Carol who backed me all the way.

We had services all over Idaho, and visited pastors everywhere giving our story. But, no more money came in. On the 26th day of our 30-day promise to the seller, the Lord spoke to my heart during the night and said, "My dear son, go in the morning to Twin Falls and wait for the blessing."

Carol and I arose early in the morning and returned to Twin Falls. Around noon we pulled into the parking lot at First Assembly and knocked on Pastor Jim Hicks' parsonage door. He nearly fell over when he saw me. "What are you doing here"?

"Well, I am here to go get the plane ready to go to Alaska. Pastor, God told me to do this. I even called ahead and had my airplane mechanic install a new ADF direction-finding radio and transponder." (This cost an additional $1,900.)

Pastor Hicks walked around in frustration. "But, we are in revival services here right now, and I haven't even been able to pay the evangelist what I had promised. Now you need $11,500!"

"Yes," I said, "but God never said it was coming from you. There is no need to be concerned."

Pastor Hicks simply threw his hand up and cried out, "God, we need a miracle!"

"Pastor Jim," I replied. "Carol and I are going out to the airplane in the morning to wash and wax it and get it ready for the trip. Would you like to come with us?" He agreed to join us.

Carol and I slept like babies that night. In the morning, Pastor Jim climbed into our pickup and off to the airport we went. What a fun day it was. We washed and waxed the plane, making it shine like a glimmering star.

The plane's owner dropped by to remind me that

we had only one more day to get the rest of the money.

"Are you worried?" I asked him. "I'm not." I truly felt that way, regardless of the outcome.

Tired, but feeling excited about Sunday services, Carol and I slept well. But Pastor Jim did not. I heard his footsteps and the yard fence creak during the night as he paced back and forth from the parsonage to the church during the night.

At 5:00 a.m., there was a sharp knock on our door. I opened the door and there was Pastor Jim, beaming from ear to ear. "Brother Rick and Carol, I don't know how God is going to do it, but He just gave me the assurance that the miracle is going to happen today!"

Though we were assured that was true, it gave us a real boost to have him confirm God's promise.

During the service, Pastor Jim shared with the congregation about the events of the past three days. Then he asked me to come to the pulpit and share some thoughts about faith. I felt like warm oil was pouring over my head as I spoke. The moment I sat down, an usher came rapidly from behind, tapped me on the shoulder, and said in a stammering voice, "Brother Rick, come to the foyer quick; I think an angel just came in here asking for you!"

An angel? I went back with the usher and there

stood a tall man dressed in shiny black shoes and a black suit. His smile overwhelmed me. In a voice soft but strong, he said, "I just stepped in and heard the last few words of your talk. Tell me, just what is it that you need?"

By this time, it felt like warm oil was again pouring all over me. I said, "What I need is $11,500 today to pay for the airplane God told me to buy for our missionary work in Alaska." His expression never changed as he said, "That is no problem." At that point, I didn't hear another word as I became lost in the Spirit.

Walking back to my seat, I turned to look back thinking the man had followed me, but he was gone. No one else saw him.

The evangelist spoke and ended the service with an altar call. After prayer, a church member and his wife came to us and said, "God spoke to us to supply your need. My wife will go with you tomorrow morning to our bank and cut you a cashier's check for that plane. May God richly bless your ministry."

I felt like a mountain lifted from my shoulders. I went to a phone and called the owner of the plane and told him what had just happened. He was silent for some time, then said, "It really looks like that plane was supposed to go to you, doesn't it?" I believe he was moved by our faith, and that the hand of God had clearly intervened on our behalf.

God does indeed work in mysterious ways His wonders to perform!

The next four days were a whirlwind of activity getting everything ready to return to Alaska. Because the Maule M-4 210 STOL (Short Take Off and Landing) airplane is considered a high-performance aircraft, I had to be qualified by a Certified Flight Instructor. It only took a little over an hour of flight time to get certified, as I had flown a number of high-performance aircraft with an instructor prior to getting the Maule.

We sold our Chevy pickup/camper as a unit for a good price. Then we flew up to McCall in our new plane. On that Saturday, we loaded all our gear into the plane. On Sunday, October 24, 1977, I spoke at Lake Fork Assembly followed by a short potluck dinner; then everyone came to the airport. Pastor Orville Scantlin dedicated the plane to the Lord and prayed over us for protection. Afterward, Carol, Dwight, and I got in the plane and everybody watched as we took off and headed for Alaska. What an amazing blessing we had experienced once again!

We flew straight to Penticton, Canada, and landed in the dark. We had to stay at the plane till we cleared customs. The trip went well overall. After a short stop in Fairbanks, we took off for Wainwright and landed safely on October 27. What a contrast in flight time from our first plane we flew from

McCall to Wainwright. That trip took 47 hours; this time only 28!

It was so good to have a plane with all the power we would ever need. The Maule was going to be such a blessing to the work in the Arctic. It was fuel injected and had a heated pitot system for determining airspeed and altitude, as well as full instrumentation for IFR flight. Also, it had a van-type rear seat which could be quickly removed. I could load 55-gallon drums or a three-wheel Honda or a small motorcycle or other oversized freight. Takeoff was very quick and short.

Our new plane had an amazingly fast cruise speed, as if pushed through the air by angels. It would fly at least 30 to 35 miles per hour faster than the Piper. Also, it needed only 200 to 300 feet of runway for takeoff. With a little headwind, I could take off in an even shorter distance. What a joy it was to return to Wainwright with this new airplane!

We made many trips to Barrow for revival services and to Eskimo camp meetings. We also flew search and rescue operations off the ice pack and traveled to winter hunting camps inland.

Emergency Rescue

One day, I flew to the Kuk River camp to take mail and pick up an injured native man. After taking off on the short, snow-covered, icy airstrip, we flew about half way to Wainwright when I noticed a lone tent with smoke rolling out the chimney. Then I saw a man waving wildly, pointing to an SOS stamped out in the snow. There was no place I could safely land close by, but I spotted a small frozen pond or lake about a quarter mile away over a small hill from the camp. I flew low over the pond a couple of times then set up for a full stall landing into the breeze on the ice.

I touched down just right and hit the brakes and the plane just slid across the ice. Then, I noticed there was about a one-foot-high bank that I hadn't seen till now. We were going to skid right into it, possibly damaging the landing gear. There wasn't enough room to take off, so I kicked full left rudder and put the plane into a sideways skid which created much more wind resistance and slowed the plane's momentum. When the plane went tail-first, sliding backward, I just gave the engine a shot of power which stopped the plane. I had never tried that before, but it worked well!

A man and woman were running toward us; the woman was carrying a very sick baby on her back inside her parka. The baby was sick with meningitis. We loaded them all into the plane and took off into the wind. I flew my passengers on to Barrow hospital. The baby recovered as did the man from the Kuk River camp. Praise the Lord!

Revival with Evangelist Warren Combs

Shortly after returning from the Kuk River camp,

Reverend Warren Combs and his wife Marjorie, former pastors at Nampa First Assembly in Idaho, flew into Barrow by jet. Carol and I flew there to pick them up in our Maule plane. It was a real introduction for them to dark Arctic winter flying! Before landing in Wainwright, we flew through a heavy snowstorm. I flew on the ADF (Automatic Direction Finder) and straight to the Wainwright DEW (Distant Early Warning) Line station that was six miles inland from the village and flew a "direct radial" to the village. After landing at Wainwright, Brother and Sister Combs just shook their heads and asked, "Do you do this all the time?"

We had great revival services for one week, Sunday through Sunday. We hung up a big, 40-foot-wide REVIVAL banner, and every evening about 30 minutes before service, Brother Combs stood on the porch steps of the church and played his trumpet loudly and beautifully. God poured out His Holy Spirit wonderfully during the meetings. Several people were saved and filled with the Holy Spirit. We also had record attendance during the last Sunday morning service. What a blessing!

Carol and I had been flying out to Meade River village about 60 miles to the southeast. We had met a Christian couple there, and since there was no church at Meade River, we would fly out and have weekly Tuesday or Thursday services in the school gym. Everyone in the village came to church. Sometimes the services would go nearly all night! Those people were so hungry for God.

We flew Brother and Sister Combs to the village for a three-day revival. When we came in for a landing, I had to accommodate a 40-mile-per-hour crosswind. For those conditions, I had developed a rather unique one-wheel, crossed-up, crab-skid landing that I could do in the M-4. But, when preparing to return to Wainwright, I could not get lined up for takeoff. The wind was so strong and the snow and ice made the runway really slick. So, I just turned the plane crossways into the wind and gave it power with full flaps, and the plane rose quickly. We got home just fine!

Whaling Adventure

As the days got longer and spring approached, I flew numerous flights with Eskimo bowhead whale hunters over the ice pack looking for the large cracks in the ice that would open up in the spring. The whales would swim up through those openings in the ice as they gathered plankton, a main source of food. Sometimes I would fly 20 to 30 miles out to sea looking for these opening in the ice. When we found a big crack that we called a "lead," we flew home and called Eskimo families on their CB radios and announced that we had found the lead, how many miles out it was, and that whales would be coming. I was always moved by the Eskimo hunters' faith in the Lord as they faithfully acknowledged the Lord by coming to the church to pray for God's favor and protection in the whale hunts.

Every able-bodied man met at the village store at 9:00 a.m. with snowmobiles, sleds, dog teams, axes, shovels, and ice picks to build an ice road to the lead. The reason a road was needed is that the ice pack would be riddled with ice presssure ridges and smaller cracks that could not be crossed over with loaded snowmobiles and sleds. So, with everyone's help, the ice road was built by using axes to lower pressure ridges and shovels to fill in the cracks with snow.

We usually built the ice road in one day. Sometimes the ice would break off close to land after everyone was at the camp set up at the lead. The wind could blow the ice out to sea with the people on it, which could create quite a challenge at times. The Eskimos would always take small boats with them as well, towing them over the ice with their snowmobiles and dogs. But, if it got very windy and stormy, the ice would begin to break up causing real danger for the people. So, sometimes, we would have to fly out and rescue people off the ice; others would escape with the small boats if the wind wasn't too bad.

When all went well, the interesting part came when hunters would shoot a whale with a large brass shoulder gun that shot a one-foot-long projectile into the whale that exploded near the heart. A strong cord was attached to the projectile and tied to a boat in case the whale began to sink. The projectile was designed to turn crossways in the whale, so, if the hunters pulled on the cord, they could hold the whale in place while they attached ropes around its tail and tow it to the edge of the ice.

The ice was always three to four feet thick at this time of year; so, to get the whale on top of the ice, the villagers used huge crowbars with ice blades on the ends to whittle the ice into a ramp down to the water. They would then drill two holes into the ice about two feet apart, some 100 feet from the edge of the ice, to wrap the large two-inch-thick nylon rope through, and then thread the rope through two large multiple pulley systems that had some four to six pulleys each. These gave them power needed to pull the whale up onto the ice for butchering.

Once the line was secured through the pulleys, then at least a hundred people would grab the rope and begin to pull. Wow! What a sight when that monstrous whale began to slide up on top of the ice! One time, however, when the Eskimos had the whale up on the ice and ran over to it, suddenly, with a roar, the ice under the whale gave way and the whale and the people close by fell into the water. That can be a major disaster as people can be crushed and drowned by large chunks of ice. But, this time, God came on the scene because the people had prayed. No one was lost! They even saved the whale. Another ramp was chiseled into the ice, and the whale was brought on top and successfully butchered.

Huge poles were used with what looked like large round and very sharp blades without teeth attached to the end. These blades made huge cuts from the top of the whale down the sides. Then ropes were attached to the large cut pieces of "muktuk," or skin and blubber, and pulled off. Everyone would grab a piece of muktuk and begin joyfully eating it raw.

A whale's skin is one to two inches thick and usually has about 12 to 18 inches of blubber beneath. Then there was all the meat--tons and tons of meat! Everything was used for various purposes--the flippers, the baleen in the whale's mouth, and the tongue which can weigh nearly a ton. It was all divided among those who helped bring in the whale according to the family size.

Everyone loaded up their portion on sleds and headed home. Most of the skeletal structure would go into the sea to feed the fish, walruses, seals, and polar bears. The whale meat went into the villagers' ice cellars dug into the permafrost.

After a successful whale hunt came the Nalakatuk Festival, a real cultural celebration with food and dancing. Included in the festivities was a blanket toss. An Eskimo would get on top of a large, round, drum-tight skin about the size of a trampoline and others would toss them high into the air. This commemorated an old method the Eskimos used to look far out into the ocean for whales. Additionally, they erected a tall flag pole with a flag reading, "Thank you, Jesus." We witnessed this throughout the six years we were in Wainwright.

Family Visits

During our years there, we also had the joy of family visits. In summer, 1975, my brother-in-law Reginald Gillatt and sister Appy Mae drove up the old Alaska Highway then flew from Fairbanks to Wainwright. While there, they conducted a two-week revival while Carol and I were in Idaho for furlough. Later, Carol's parents, Ted and Mary Maenpa, flew to Barrow where we met them and flew them to Wainwright for a two-week visit. They really enjoyed the Arctic Ocean, the sound of walruses, and watching whales spout. Also, my parents, Art and Appy Rigenhagen, flew up in fall 1979 to help me build a sloped roof on the parsonage that previously had been flat and leaky. That was probably my father's last major job before retiring. He was pleased to serve the Lord by helping us with this project.

Though many more stories could be told of our six years in Wainwright, God set things in motion for another transition that would soon take place.

Shaktoolik

While at an Eskimo camp meeting in Barrow in late winter 1979, God spoke to my heart about moving to the village of Shaktoolik located on the west coast of Alaska. Carol and I were torn in many ways, as we so loved Wainwright. Also, I didn't know how moving there could happen since a missionary already resided in Shaktoolik. However, on May 9, 1980, Carol and I and two ladies from Wainwright flew to Shaktoolik for their Eskimo camp meeting. While there, God confirmed in my heart that I would be serving there as pastor. I didn't say anything to others about it at the time.

As soon as we returned to Wainwright, I received a phone call from our superintendent Willard Leisy who said to me, "Brother Rick, you have had six wonderful years in Wainwright, haven't you?"

"Yes, we have really enjoyed our time here, and God has really blessed," I replied.

Then he blew me away by saying, "God spoke to me to move you to Shaktoolik. Would you be willing to terminate your time in Wainwright and take this new mission?" I choked and cried realizing that again God had confirmed our calling. Sobbing, I said, "Yes, Brother Leisy, God already spoke to me over a month ago, but I just didn't know how that was going to happen."

"Brother Potter is moving to another mission," Leisy replied. "I would like you to move to Shaktoolik in a month." Wow! That started a whirlwind of activity as we resigned as pastor at Wainwright, had a moving sale, and packed and mailed 52 boxes of our belongings. There were lots of tears, hugs, and cards from the people we had come to love so much.

We flew into Shaktoolik on June 13, 1980. Now some 180 miles south of the Arctic Circle, instead of 300 miles north of it, the weather was more moderate. The sun never totally left, the summers came earlier, and winters were significantly shorter. But, being on the coast of the Bering Sea, about 180 miles from Siberia, we got a lot of windy and wet weather.

The parsonage and church were side by side and quite new. We had running water from about mid-April through the second week of October. We also had a flushing toilet and a washer and dryer. When running water wasn't available, we washed clothes at the village laundromat. During the winter, we hauled our own water in 5- to 10-gallon plastic jugs till the pipelines thawed; still it was much easier and milder than in Wainwright.

Milder temperatures and warmer summer brought wild flowers and wild berries of all sorts. Salmon berries, wild blueberries, low-bush cranberries, and wild strawberries were plentiful. Fishing was a fisherman's dream! King salmon, red salmon, humpies (pink salmon), Dolly Varden trout, and herring also were plentiful. Though there were no roads within 600 miles, numerous commercial freezer ship companies came and bought fish from the natives.

Carol and I had received a 35-horsepower Johnson outboard jet motor from Speed-the-Light; so, we went to Unalakleet and bought a 12-foot, flat-bottomed river boat. Lightly loaded, that boat could navigate in only four inches of water; however, I didn't dare stop till I got into a foot or more of water; otherwise, I would bottom out and have to pack the boat out.

Royal Rangers Adventures

Not long after moving to Shaktoolik, we established the first Royal Rangers outpost in the village. Ted Walden, state Royal Rangers Commander from Anchorage, few with me to our village to assist us in getting the outpost started. We took the boys several miles up the Shaktoolik River and camped in grizzly bear territory along the river near the mountains. Because of the grizzlies, the leaders were approved to carry 12-guage magnum shotguns for protection if needed.

On the first night, after a really wonderful campfire dinner of fresh-caught fish and pork and beans, we had a very spiritual time with the Lord. Then we went to our tents for the night.

Around midnight, we were suddenly awakened by cracking willows and loud growling right near our tents. Ted was in a different tent than I, but we both grabbed our shotguns and flashlights and jumped out of our tents to protect the boys. Soon, all the boys were out of their tents clinging to each other in fright. Then one of the boys jumped out of the brush laughing, "Ha! Did I scare you?"

Needless to say, Ted and I were very upset. We both grabbed the boy, and, in front of the other Rangers, we had a very direct, eye-to-eye talk with the prankster. Before he had jumped out of the brush, both Ted and I had our shotguns trained in his direction. Thankfully, neither of us pulled the trigger. That young man was immediately assigned to KP duty with limited privileges.

We were geared up to stay for four days but encountered a problem. Every boy was to bring enough food rations for four days. However, each of the boys brought several cans of pork and beans and not much of anything else. After two and a half day we headed home. None of the boys could stand being zipped up in their tents together! But, beans and grizzlies aside, those boys became good Royal Rangers and honorable young men. In fact, our resident "grizzly" would go on to the state Royal Rangers Pow-Wow and receive runner-up as Royal Ranger of the Year!

The Royal Rangers Pow-Wow was held about 110 miles northeast of the Alaska Range. I flew three of our top boys to the camp. During our flight, the air became very turbulent; and to make matters worse, area forest fires filled the air with smoke. Soon, one of the boys got really sick to the stomach and was about to throw up. So, I handed him one of those special bags used in planes for such occasions, and he proceeded to fill it. After he tied it nicely, I asked him to hand it to me and I would toss it out the window. But as soon as he handed it to me, we hit turbulence again and the bottom of the bag opened spilling the contents over all of us. Now we were all sick with not enough bags to go around! What a trip!

We eventually made it to the mountain landing strip near camp, and I put the boys to work with Pine Sol and water to clean up the mess; but it still smelled pretty bad on the way home. But, despite all that, our boys were the pride of the village. At every village event, the city leaders would have our Rangers open with prayer and serve as the honor guard to post the U.S. flag.

Special Visitors

Not long before we had come to Shaktoolik, the church began hosting an annual Eskimo camp meeting that lasted a full week from Sunday to Sunday. We invited Rev. Homer Walkup and his wife Rachel to come to Shaktoolik to be our camp meeting evangelists. Brother Walkup had recently retired as Southern Idaho District Superintendent. He and Rachel flew into Unalakleet in a 737 jet, then I picked them up in our Maule airplane and flew them to Shaktoolik. For the services, around a hundred people flew in from villages all around the area, and local people took them into their homes for the week. Many people were saved, baptized in the Holy Spirit, and healed.

During that week, Carol and I flew the Walkup's to Nome and to other villages around the area, so they could experience the local culture and foods. I definitely wanted them to taste muktuk, whale blubber, herring eggs, kelp salad, as well as outdoor-smoked fish.

During a flight over Norton Sound, we came upon many large seals sunning themselves around holes in the ice. En route back to Fairbanks, from where the Walkup's would return home, we flew through Rainy Pass in the Alaska Range and saw ocean glaciers. Off to our left, Mt. McKinley towered more than 12,000 feet above our 9,000-foot altitude. Oh, the grandeur of God's creation!

Before reaching Fairbanks, we landed at Willow to visit Missionaries Ken and Ethel Andrus. Earlier, Ken and I had discussed trading airplanes straight across. He had a really nice, low-air-time, 235 Piper

Cherokee with tundra tires and an 84-gallon fuel capacity. I really needed more fuel range. The Maule could only carry 40 gallons of fuel which allowed only about three hours of flight; the 235 would allow six-plus hours. The Piper also was quite a bit larger and roomier, as well as quieter, and could fly about 10 miles-per-hour faster. After finalizing arrangements for the swap, I checked out in the 235, then off we went to Fairbanks.

Brother Walkup spoke for services at Fairbanks First Assembly and at our church in North Pole. Afterward, they returned to Idaho. They had really enjoyed their trip to Alaska.

Following one of our first trips to Fairbanks for supplies and for services at First Assembly, Alaska District Superintendent Edward Hughes flew back to Shaktoolik with us. He was always such a blessing to us during our years in Alaska. Staying a couple of weeks, Brother Hughes visited a number of our west coast villages. I flew him to Nome, St. Michael, Emmonak, Unalakleet, and McGrath, to visit the missionaries and pastors in those remote villages. His greatest joy, however, was to ride our little flat-bottomed jet boat up the Shaktoolik River and fish. He got so excited I thought he might be raptured. Every time his lure hit the water, he caught a fish. He caught over 60 fish in less than two hours! We bagged them up and put them in the freezer. When it was time to fly him back to Fairbanks, we just wrapped the fish in newspaper and put them in a cardboard box and loaded them into the luggage compartment.

Search and Rescue

While in Shaktoolik, I again became involved with search and rescue operations looking for downed airplanes, lost boats, and hunters. Often, when bad weather moved in, planes would go down in the mountains close by; boaters would lose course and get lost. So, I would load the plane with spotters carrying binoculars. I had to fly low, up and down the canyons and over mountains. I flew over Norton Sound for lost boaters or float planes. Only one search was unsuccessful. Ryan Air founder and owner went down in a bad storm on his way to Nome. We searched in vain for weeks. Sometime in the spring, he was found on a mountainside. In all likelihood, he had perished instantly.

Sometimes search and rescue was a very sobering experience. It was always tragic to find a charred spot where a plane had violently crashed or to see a tangled pile of aluminum that had been a beautiful airplane. Having to report, "We just found the missing plane, but see no survivors," was gut wrenching. Successful operations, however, were so different. It was wonderful to see people waving and jumping around when we located a downed plane or lost boat. Sometimes people had been lost for days. On many occasions, I would drop emergency supplies—food, blankets, first aid supplies—to help the survivors to be more comfortable until a rescue helicopter, land team, or the Coast Guard could reach them.

One thing I learned was that an urgent rescue often opened hearts of people who were potentially unfriendly or even hostile. It was wonderful to get hugs and see the tears of otherwise unapproachable people. They would almost always open up spiritually and in other ways, aware that we had risked our lives to save them. Only eternity will reveal just how much was done. Thankfully, however, urgent rescues were quite rare.

Berries and Bears

One beautiful sunny summer day, Carol and I and a local church member named Emma got in our flat-bottomed jet boat to go up a shallow slough that went serveral miles inland toward the mountains where we would find great blueberry patches. We had packed a lunch, and I took my .30-.30 rifle and .44 magnum pistol. The guns were a precaution as we were going into an area populated by grizzly bears. When we arrived, sure enough, there were very fresh tracks in the mud along the bank of the slough.

We stopped and listened. It was eerily quiet, so we climbed up the bank and made our way to the berry patch. And, wow, what beautiful, big blueberries, and so many of them! But after picking for about 30 minutes, nearby we heard a deep, muffled growl and shaking willows. What little hair I had stood straight up!

Emma said, "Let's get out of here now!" So, we got close together, backed away from the willows, and moved toward the boat. My guns were at the ready. The bear never showed himself, but he sure made noise. Despite the scare, we were very happy with the blueberries we had picked. Blueberries with sugar and cream and a cup of coffee were a delicious treat, not to mention the blueberry pie and cobbler. My, it was good!

Our son Dwight, who was 14 at the time, sold his childhood toys and did odd jobs around the village to buy a Yamaha 80 dirt bike. I also purchased a Yamaha 175 dirt bike. Carol, Dwight, and I loved to make trips up the beach on our motorcycles. Shaktoolik was on the Bering Sea and there was very little mud, mostly gravel and sand. We could ride for miles, being ever mindful, of course, to watch out for grizzlies!

Ongoing Mission and Vision

Through Speed-the-Light, we were able to secure a three-wheeled, fat-tire Honda and a fat-tired trailer to transport our Royal Rangers on outings closer to the village. We also used it to haul supplies and gasoline to and from the airport, and to transport people to the airport for our missions trips. Additionally, we received a snowmobile and sled to use for the same reasons during the long winters. We were able to haul firewood in from the timber about a mile inland. Speed-the-Light was such a blessing to us in helping us to get the gospel out to precious people!

We flew a number of our Shaktoolik people to Nome for winter Eskimo camp meeting. The native people love to get together at these meetings. At Nome, I met several Spirit-filled Presbyterian people from St. Lawrence Island who also had flown in. They were excited about the possibility of our coming to their island to have services and to eventually build an Assemblies of God mission.

I realized now that the calling I had felt from the beginning of our missionary work seemed to be falling into place. However, before I could begin an outreach to St. Lawrence Island, I would need a different aircraft, particularly a Geronimo Apache with high-performance twin engines and equipped with survival gear for regular over-water operations. When I shared this vision with the national Assemblies of God U.S. Missions office and the Alaska District office, they were very interested in this idea. However, we were still very involved in Shaktoolik and other coastal village outreaches. So, St. Lawrence Island was put on hold for the time being. I told the people to pray that God would put that part of the calling into action in His time.

Outreach Ministries

We began a winter, village-wide youth game night in our parsonage basement. We set up two, side-by-side ping pong tables and had several table box games available along with coffee, hot chocolate, cookies, etc. That really brought our village youth together and got them away from drug and alcohol activities that so dominated many lives. We also had fellowship potluck dinners and ping pong playoffs. It really helped bring the village people together.

We also enjoyed wonderful fellowship with the Covenant Christian Church in the village. We began attending their get-togethers, and I flew many of their members, along with ours, to social events in other villages.

Due to this relationship, in the midst of a tragic circumstance, I was asked to preach the Koyuk village Covenant get-together where some 400 people had flown in from all along the west coast. Tragically, a 12-year-old son of the evangelist they had flown in for services drowned the first day in a natural hot spring pool. Though the situation was difficult to understand, I was greatly honored to take the place of their evangelist. On the first night, I preached on "The Trials of Life." After the message, I asked the people to come forward to pray over their pastor. When they did, the Holy Spirit began to fall on everyone, and the people began to cry out to God for more of the Holy Spirit's power in their lives. It was so wonderful to see the walls break down and sense the oneness of the Spirit that came out of those meetings.

After returning home from Koyuk, I received a

phone call from the Covenant Christian radio station in Nome to send them a weekly, 30-minute tape from our church services. Wow! Were we ever blessed! God had opened many new ministry opportunities during those days, and, as a result, we saw numerous miracles of healing and Holy Spirit baptisms.

Search for a Hunting Party

One very blustery spring day after the ice breakup, I was visited by several village men that were very concerned about a hunting party that had gone out to sea four days prior. They had not returned, nor had they contacted anyone by shortwave radio. The ocean was too violent for them to survive in a boat. The men begged me to fly out to a small island several miles off the coast to see if they might have made it to the island.

I knew I would be well outside the conditions for a safe flight. The weather was really bad. Ground winds were clocked at 40 to 50 miles per hour, and I knew that over the ocean, around the island, the winds would likely exceed 60 miles per hour. But, the men's insistence, urgency, and willingness to join me in the plane caused me to take a chance on the flight.

Takeoff went well, but as soon as we were airborne, I knew we were in for quite a ride. The plane bucked like a stallion. However, after climbing to around 2,000 feet, the turbulence lessened. Yet, the waves below told me we would get hammered as we approached the island. If the men were on the island, they would be on the lee side of a huge mountain cliff to gain protection from the winds. When I descended to scan the coves along the beach, a severe downdraft caught the plane. To compensate, I slowed to slightly under 100 miles per hour and went to full power to maintain altitude. The slower speed softened the blows on the wings somewhat.

As we scanned the coves, we were greatly relieved to spot the men who were safe and sound. They signaled to us they were okay, so, I pulled away from the cliff going out to sea and climbed back to 2,000 feet where the air was smoother. At that point I noticed that my forehead and hands were wet with perspiration. But what a relief for the concerned families! We all gave thanks to the Lord.

Transition to Come

Though we loved ministering in Shaktoolik, our finances had declined significantly. In Wainwright, Carol provided child care for the village school teachers and I worked part-time for the village corporation to supplement our income. However, very little work was available in Shaktoolik. We just couldn't keep up with the airplane expenses. So, we were approved to go to church districts outside our home district for itinerary to raise additional budget. Another missionary family just coming to Alaska would be able to fill in for us in Shaktoolik while we would be away for the next year.

We loaded up our Cherokee with baggage in August and took off again for Idaho. What a difference in speed and comfort in the Cherokee. With its long fuel range, we had to land far less often. Overall, it took less than 17 hours flying time to make it to McCall versus 47 hours in the PA-20, and 28 hours in the Maule. We loved the Cherokee. It proved its worth in reliability, load-carrying ability, and extreme cold weather operation; and it was much more stable in severe turbulence.

Our itinerary went well; we even used our plane for some of the longer distance services. During our travels, we were surprised and shocked by a phone call from our Alaska District Superintendent who asked us to take the mission at Fort Yukon when we returned, and, from there, fly a ministry circuit among five other villages. This was certainly an unexpected change. We did not feel that our calling was over at Shaktoolik, and this would also mean further delaying outreach ministry to St. Lawrence Island.

"We need you to take this mission," our superintendent stated. "The missionaries who came to fill in at Shaktoolik want to stay."

At first, Carol and I were heartbroken. But, as we prayed, God assured us that we needed to obey those in authority over us, and that He would bless our work there. What a change this would be.

Additionally, there was the matter of transporting all our belongings at Shaktoolik. There were no roads for 600 miles.

On one of our flights while in Idaho, Carol and I took her parents over some really beautiful mountain country to visit my brother Art and wife Marcy in Idaho City. We would also have a service at the Assembly of God church there. My father and mother drove up from Star to be with us as well. It turned out to be a great family reunion.

I was surprised when, after we had exited the plane, my mother climbed into the back seat and said, "Well, aren't you going to take me for a ride with you, Son?" I laughed and asked if anyone else wanted to go. My brother Art, Dad, and a lady from the church jumped in. We took off and flew back up a canyon to view an old gold claim we had back in the mountains. Mother was very excited. I know that flight calmed her nerves about our flying in the Alaska bush.

After that trip, Carol and I flew to Twin Falls for services at First Assembly and Faith Assembly. While there, we also needed to have an annual inspection done on our plane.

A Slow Journey Home

We drove our pickup and camper to Wyoming for a few missionary services. While at the Assembly of God church in Dubois, pastored by Clifford Scheline, we received a call from a dear lady we had met at Walter Buck's church in Spokane, Washington. She told me that her husband had just passed away from a heart attack. He had been in the process of remodeling an 8- by 42-foot house trailer and had nearly completed it before he died.

"I want to give that trailer to you," she said. "Maybe you can tow it back to Alaska and live in it if needed or sell it."

We decided to take her up on her most gracious offer. So, on our return to Alaska, we hooked the trailer to our 1981 Ford F150, 4 X 4, and headed up the Alaska Highway. However, the pickup had only a 300-cubic-inch, six-cylinder engine with a four-speed transmission, and the trailer weighed 14,000 pounds. So, we were severely overloaded.

En route, the pickup would do only about 45 to 50 miles-per-hour and was getting only about six miles per gallon. When I came to a hill, I would have to shift down to first gear and grind up the hill. Going downhill, I didn't dare get rolling too fast or the brakes would get hot, start smoking, and quit holding. So, I had to grind in low gear downhill as well, much to the chagrin of people trying to get around us on the steep, winding roads. I pulled over anytime there was a wide spot in the road.

In addition to the painstakingly slow progress, we blew five tires and then the rear end went out near Fort Nelson, British Columbia. Thankfully, the Pentecostal Assemblies of Canada helped us out with a service and an offering to help cover expenses. What a relief it was when we finally pulled into Fairbanks. It had been a long and arduous journey!

Don Nelson, manager of KJNP, a 50,000-watt Christian radio station, called me and said, "Rick, sell your trailer and move into our KJNP house in Fort Yukon. You need to live there instead of flying out from Fairbanks all the time." What a blessing! So, that is what we decided to do. Shortly afterward, a man came by and gave us a good price for the trailer.

We flew out to Fort Yukon on Air North Airlines and got our house set up for living. Then, I had to fly via commercial airline back to Twin Falls, Idaho, to get our Cherokee. That was the first time I would fly the Alaska Highway route alone. I took off from Twin Falls and flew to McCall to get the rest of our supplies and to visit Ted and Mary Maenpa. I stayed overnight and left early on September 23, 1981.

I felt very much alone as I approached the Canadian border. My loneliness, however, was suddenly interrupted by a loud noise and banging sound coming from the engine, plus a terrible smell. I was over mountains, and, as always, I was scanning the horizon for emergency landing places. Toward the south, I noticed a large farm and what looked like a small airstrip. I had 8,500 feet altitude, so I cut power way back and started a long descent toward the airstrip.

The noise coming from the engine compartment was not good! It smelled like the plane was on fire. I prayed as I descended, lined up on the little strip, and landed. Then, I spotted an agricultural spray plane and a man walking toward me. Amazingly, the man not only owned the large ranch with his own spray plane, but he also had a nice shop with lots of tools and airplane parts!

When we looked at the engine, we discovered that the whole exhaust system had dropped off the engine and was just lying at the bottom of the cowling. The mechanic that had installed the exhaust system during inspection failed to tighten the manifold bolts; all of them had fallen off. Altogether, I needed six exhaust gaskets and 12 exhaust nuts and washers. The ranch owner had them all! Praise the Lord! He didn't even charge me for them when he learned I was a missionary.

How amazingly God had again watched over me and orchestrated the provision of every need in such detail. I thanked the rancher for his gracious help and took off. The rest of the trip went smoothly. It was a great joy to land at Fort Yukon and hug my family!

Fort Yukon

We started getting things set up in earnest as winter comes early at Fort Yukon, which is situated eight miles north of the Arctic Circle. We also learned that things could be a bit exciting at times. One day as Carol was outside hanging clothes on the clothesline, she heard a noise and turned around just in time to see a large bear running at full speed, being chased by a guy on a four-wheeler. The bear was only about 50 feet from her when it ran by! Carol's heart pounded like a drum. We found out this would not be an uncommon event.

Carol and I jogged a lap around the airport each day for exercise. However, I always carried a high-caliber weapon when walking or jogging as a precaution.

After getting settled in, we were anxious to visit all of the five villages we would be serving. Stevens was about 125 miles west on the banks of the Yukon River; Beaver was some 60 miles up the banks of the Yukon; Birch Creek was only about 25 miles southwest; Chalkyitsik was some 60 miles east; and, finally, Circle was 50 miles up the Yukon

River.

Before visiting the villages, however, we needed to fly back to Shaktoolik to gather up things to send to Fort Yukon and sell or give away other things. We left the Speed-the-Light boat motor, snowmobile, and three-wheeled Honda for the missionaries there. It truly was hard to leave Shaktoolik so soon, but we were anxious to get settled in Fort Yukon and begin our full-time circuit-flying mission.

Flying the Circuit

We officially began our village flying circuit on October 17, 1982. Stevens Village had a small log church and a two-room cabin for the parsonage. Since winter was coming on strong and we had to heat with wood, we decided not to heat both the church and parsonage as it would take a large amount of wood; and wood was in pretty short supply at the time. Since there were only about ten people in the congregation, we decided to have services in the parsonage. Congregation members would bring a few blocks of wood for heat.

Carol and I usually stayed overnight when ministering in the villages, as there were no runway lights for a nighttime takeoff. We brought food with us and put a catalytic heater or another heat source in the airplane cowling overnight. It could be furiously cold sometimes. On one occasion, it was minus 64 degrees at Beaver village. But did we ever have wonderful services! At Chalkytsik village, the Episcopal priest became Spirit-filled and would bring a crowd to our little mission. Sometimes the services went for hours as people hungered for the Holy Spirit in their lives.

Raleigh Ferrell, national secretary of Assemblies of God U.S. Missions in Springfield, Missouri, flew up with Alaska Superintendent Jack Bransford to view some of our remote mission stations. While we were sitting around our table for breakfast in our KJNP cabin, the phone rang. It was the district office secretary informing us that missionary pilot Ken Andrus had just been killed in his plane at Nuiqsut village. I was stunned. Ken had been flying the Maule we traded for the Cherokee we were now flying. Trying to land in bad weather, Ken flew into a large, frozen dirt bank and was killed instantly. I loved him as a brother, so this news was very upsetting to me personally. But, after brothers Bransford and Ferrell prayed with Carol and me, I was able to fly with confidence despite the terrible news.

Brother Ferrell was amazed at how tough it was just to live in the Arctic with no running water or flushing toilets, no electricity to heat the planes, and no runway lights, not to mention that minus 40 degrees could be considered a nice day! But, it gave him a true picture of what ministering was like in the remote villages.

While in Fort Yukon, Don Nelson from the radio

station loaned us a little white Volkswagen bug that had a unique gas heater. It used gas from the car's tank and functioned like a compact gas furnace. Some models even had a duct into the engine compartment to preheat the engine on cold days. They worked like heaters on airplanes. It was wonderful to turn on that gas heater, as it delivered lots of warmth instantly.

Don also let us use a one-and-a-half-ton truck to haul firewood. Later, a man from Fairbanks First Assembly gave us a nice three-quarter-ton Chevy pickup that turned out to be a real blessing. I was able to haul fuel for the plane as well as firewood.

Carol started baby-sitting for some school teachers in the village which helped us out financially. It cost a lot to keep the plane airworthy. We just could not raise enough money in pledges to fully support the work; but, somehow, God always came through for us.

We were always amazed at how God directed us and met our needs in answer to prayer. He doesn't always meet our needs just the way we want; and sometimes He works in mysterious ways, His wonders to perform!

As an amazing example of God's provision, I was approached by the manager of an Alaska Commercial Company store who asked if I would consider working at their marine, snowmobile, and Honda shop as their mechanic and service manager.

The pay would be wonderful; however, I was concerned that it would limit flying our circuit to the villages. The manager assured me that I could have days off pretty much whenever I needed them for our missionary work. So, I accepted the job and soon discovered that God had provided a wonderful opportunity. Most of the people from the villages that we visited bought a lot of their boat, snowmobile, and Honda ATV parts and service at my shop. So, I got to meet lots of native people and became very close to many of them and ministered to them.

Engine Trouble

Missionary Dave Wilson who pastored the native Assembly of God in Fairbanks, had flown out to Fort Yukon with me and was going to speak at a Saturday night service with us at Chalkytksik village. We had to fly out before dark, as they had no landing lights on the runway. The Episcopal priest who had been filled with the Holy Spirit, invited us to have the service in his large house. What a service we had!

Around 11:00 p.m., we took off from the village, using the powerful landing lights on the Cherokee to light the reflectors that lined the runway. As soon as we were airborne, I homed in on the Fort Yukon VOR and ADF frequencies and flew instrument. But, about halfway there, the engine suddenly began to run very rough and vibrate badly. That is bad enough during the daylight when you can see the terrain, but on a dark night it becomes a very serious problem.

I discovered that if I throttled back to about 40 to 50 percent power, with the constant-speed hydraulic prop set at 1,800 rpms, the vibrating settled down pretty well and we could maintain altitude. Finally, we saw the beacon at Fort Yukon, and we soon landed safely. After inspecting the engine, we discovered that its life was nearly spent. The engine had almost 1,800 hours of hard use in the Arctic that exacts a high toll on airplane engines.

Blessed by CAP

In all the villages we ministered in, I had some limited involvement with the Civil Air Patrol (CAP), by being engaged in various searches that involved local law enforcement and working with search and rescue teams. When we moved to Fort Yukon, there was immediate need for qualified search and rescue pilots and spotters. CAP leaders remembered my flying experience and successes with searches. So, in addition to flying missions, I was asked to serve as chaplain for the CAP unit and to help train cadets through which I earned credits toward the eventual rank of second lieutenant. My training in specially equipped Cessna Skyhawks was received primarily at Eielson Air Force Base in North Pole. I also became qualified to fly my own aircraft in CAP searches.

For the time being, however, our ministry was

pretty much at a standstill until we could get another engine for our plane. But God had another plan that was directly linked to my involvement CAP.

One day, the CAP commander contacted me and said, "Since you are our chaplain and have a second lieutenant officer rating, just wear your CAP uniform and fly one of our airplanes to your villages and promote CAP along with your chaplaincy duties."

What an amazing offer! So, I flew a CAP Skyhawk to the villages until our plane was repaired. The repair cost for our plane, however, was significant, which was another concern.

About two weeks later, Pastor Roland Peretti from North Pole Assembly of God, called and said, "God told me to have you come next Sunday morning to speak for us. Can you make it?" I accepted the invitation. I spoke on Sunday morning, and after the offering was taken, they handed me a check for the exact amount that we needed to fix our plane! God is so good! If He calls you, He will meet your needs.

Promise in the Sky

God's ever-present care proved to be true throughout our missionary service in Alaska. Another instance relates to a time when I flew a missionary evangelist family to Chalkytsik village for services the next summer. They stayed for two weeks and really had a revival! Many people were saved and filled with the Spirit.

At the conclusion of their services, I flew from Fort Yukon to pick them up and fly them over the White Mountain Range into Fairbanks. Though the weather was questionable, the evangelist was on a tight schedule and had to get to Fairbanks. So, I belted his wife and two children in the back seats, and he climbed in beside me. Soon after takeoff, as we were climbing to cruise altitude of 8,000 feet, it started to rain. The farther we flew, the harder it rained. I was concerned that torrential rain might drown the engine. Then the turbulence started and became increasingly severe, but the evangelist wanted to continue, believing God had ordained so.

We prayed, but the sky got darker and darker. I was beginning to sweat when, suddenly, we broke out of the storm. Though we were under a very dark overcast, the sun was shining on us from the west in the late evening. Then, amazingly, a glorious, brilliantly colored rainbow surrounded us! I had never seen anything like it in all my life. The rainbow seemed to move with us. Every direction I looked, straight up, to the left, the right, straight down, we were surrounded by this unbelievably beautiful colorful circle of God's promise and beauty. All fear left us, and we began to lift our hearts in praise unto the Lord! We soon landed safely in Fairbanks.

Our circuit flying mission seemed to be going well. All the villages were small, but they were our places of ministry each week. Carol and I would fly out to Stevens village on Saturday night and stay overnight in the log cabin parsonage to heat the building for services on Sunday morning. I would use various means to keep the plane engine warm till it was time to take off for Beaver's Sunday night service.

We usually flew back in the dark from Beaver to Fort Yukon, which was only 60 miles. I always had to take off in the dark using the plane's landing lights as there were no runway lights. On one very cold night, when I started the plane, the landing lights didn't work. So, I just held my five-cell flashlight out the window as we took off. I prayed that the Fort Yukon runways lights would be working, and they were. Praise the Lord!

Arctic Circle "Bump"

We covered the other three villages during the week as weather allowed. I really enjoyed having some of the native people, who were on fire for the Lord, fly with me to the villages to give their testimonies.

As time approached for another Eskimo winter camp meeting, I received a phone call from our Superintendent, Jack Bransford. He asked if I would fly to McGrath and pick him up along with Robert Pirtle, national director of Assemblies of God U.S.

Missions. The superintendent wanted to take Brother Pirtle on a tour of several west-coast village missions. Then we would go back to Nome where Pirtle was scheduled to preach the camp meeting.

After checking the weather along the route, I knew this was going to be a challenging journey, but they were willing to give it a try. So, I took off for McGrath which is about 240 miles down the Yukon valley, across the Kuskokwim Mountains. That leg of the trip went well, so I fueled up, ate lunch, picked up Pirtle and Bransford, and took off for Saint Michael's village to visit Missionary Dave Wilson. But, over the Kaiyah Mountains we began picking up ice, so we diverted to Shaktoolik village and had a service there.

The next morning, we took off for Kotzebue. The weather looked good, but the forecast indicated that a strong Arctic storm was moving in from Siberia and would arrive in the morning when we wanted to fly back to Nome.

As we continued to Kotzebue, Brother Bransford leaned forward and whispered in my ear, "Give Robert the 'Arctic Circle Bump' when we cross the Circle." So, about 30 miles south of Kotzebue, I directed Brother Pirtle's attention to something on the ground, then I quickly shoved on the controls forward. Our bellies came up to our throats momentarily, and I shouted, "Wow! That was a powerful Arctic Circle bump!" Pirtle had a really puzzled look on his face and said, "I wonder what causes that?" Brother Bransford had a really good laugh.

After landing, I fueled the plane and tied it down securely. Missionary James Schulz then picked us up at the airport in his Speed-the-Light suburban and took us into Kotzebue, a town built on the end of a 40-mile spit of sand and gravel that juts out into the Arctic Ocean. It's almost always windy there. Brother Schulz had built a nice church and parsonage in the village, and we had a great evening service with the church folk there.

Sure enough, as forecasted, the morning brought a powerful wind, snow, and ice that would be around for a few days. To make matters worse, I awoke with a rotten cold and flu. So, I would not be piloting anywhere for a while without a real miracle. Since I couldn't fly, Brothers Bransford and Pirtle flew out on a Wein jet to Nome, and I stayed in bed for three or four days. After the storm and flu subsided, I took off for Fort Yukon.

Sky Evangelism

Later that summer, missionary aviator Mike Hines from Latin America was home on furlough. He flew his highly modified Helio Courier to Alaska to have services around the native villages and demonstrate his unusual method of preaching the gospel to entire towns and cities from the air. Hines had purchased one of only seven powerful military airborne sound systems that were used during the Vietnam War to frighten the enemy or warn Vietnamese communities of impending military actions. Sound was projected through a large, aerodynamic door that opened on the left side of the plane while flying.

The plane was powered by a TGO-490, turbocharged Lycoming engine. With the prop speed turned way down, and the turbocharger at a low setting, Hines could fly low and quietly circle a village. With the plane on automatic pilot, he could then preach, play music, and have altar calls from the air. The speaker system was so powerful it could put 80-plus decibels of undistorted sound on the ground from two to three miles away!

Flying with him over our villages, I saw firsthand just how effective it was. Many people fell to their knees in the streets, giving their hearts to Jesus! Sometimes angry atheists or other antagonists would shoot at the plane. Hines' plane had patches on the wing where a man in South America made several bullet holes with a machine gun.

When it was time for Mike to leave Fort Yukon, he climbed above the clouds and turned on a recording of "The King Is Coming!" complete with loud cymbals, drum rolls, and a massive choir. When a backslidden man working on the roof of his house heard the choir singing from the clouds, he thought Jesus was coming and he was going to be left behind. He fell off the ladder and landed on the ground, unharmed, thankfully. We hope we will see him in heaven one day.

Fort Yukon Pastorate

After we had been doing the circuit from Fort Yukon for two years, the pastor of the Fort Yukon Assembly of God church resigned. The Alaska District sent the presbyter to have a meeting with the members of the church. They voted 100 percent for us to take that church, allowing that we would still fly the village circuit during weekdays.

We moved into the large, beautiful parsonage that had been built by Pastor Ron Faust. The house had 12-inch-thick, insulated walls. Both the church and parsonage were atop a small hill, out of the flood plain. There was a 1,000-gallon water tank in the basement, a flushing toilet, and a washer and dryer. Also, we had a septic tank that worked! Additionally, there was a 300-gallon water tank mounted on the back of a truck to haul water for the mission from the city water plant by the river.

The parsonage also featured a combination wood/oil, hot water-circulating furnace. The system heated the house well but used lots of wood and stove oil. When the wood fire burned out, the oil gun in the firebox would take over heating the water. But, the creosote created by the burning wood lowered the efficiency of the system.

Additionally, the church owned an old, one-ton, Chevy flatbed truck that we used to haul wood for the church and parsonage. Also, I had a 20-foot, flat-bottomed boat to haul firewood and to use for visiting hunting and fishing camps up and down the Yukon and Porcupine Rivers.

On Wednesday nights, we had our prayer and Bible study service in the parsonage to keep from having to warm the church during cold weather. We also were blessed to have a heated car garage. I installed an insulated, folding overhead electric/wireless door opener. What a blessing!

AIM Outreach

One summer, I was contacted by the Colorado District youth director who wanted to set up an Ambassadors in Mission (AIM) trip. He and eight of his youth would fly out to our villages to conduct Vacation Bible Schools (VBS). I advised him that this would be a pretty rugged trip for city youth as there would be no running water, flushing toilets, or showers, except in our home village of Fort Yukon. He assured me that would be okay.

I would deliver the young people to the villages and get them oriented to their week of VBS and their living conditions. Afterward, I would have to leave them and get the other teams set up in their villages. We had agreed on serving the villages of Stevens, Beaver, and Fort Yukon.

After flying the youth to the villages, I introduced them to the native helpers and kids to whom they would be ministering. I also got their food and supplies in place for the week. Ann Stout, a cousin of mine from Fort Collins Assembly in Colorado, plus one of her friends, were assigned to Fort Yukon.

My greatest concerns in the remote areas were bears, possible moose attacks, and other injuries. There was no doctor for some 140 miles. But, truly, the Lord blessed these young people. The native children and families told me of the great VBS programs and how the youth ministered to the adults in the evenings. Thankfully, also, there were no illnesses or injuries. To God be the glory!

Airplane Trade

Carol and I began to think that we should downsize our airplane, as the big 235 Cherokee was expensive to maintain and burned over 12 gallons of fuel per hour. A man in Anchorage offered to trade for a Piper Cherokee 140 that was three years newer and had a four-cylinder, 150-horsepower engine. It also had a nice radio and IFR instrument navigation package. Carol and I felt we should go for it and we did so.

I flew our Cherokee to Anchorage, made the swap for the Piper, and flew back home. It took me about an hour longer to fly back from Anchorage to Fort Yukon than it would have taken in the 235. Also, the Piper had a smaller cabin, was noisier, and had only a 600-mile range; but, we were confident that, overall, it would be more economical to fly.

Shortly after the trade, I had a Bush STOL (short takeoff and landing) kit installed by Reverend Lee Wiles in Anchorage. It made the plane handle better in both takeoffs and landings on short fields. Also, I picked up a few more miles per hour as well. Additionally, the kit made the plane look nice with drooped wingtips, stall fences and high-lift leading edge cuffs on the wings, and a larger vertical stabilizer from the rudder down to the fuselage. Overall, I had to admit that the 140 would be great for the short hops to the five villages. We made countless flights for funerals, weddings, church services, and visiting the sick.

In the spring, Don Nelson, general manager of the KJNP radio station in North Pole, would fly out to Fort Yukon checking the status of ice breakup on the Yukon River. We would fly up and down the river, watching for dangerous ice jams that might flood the villages. Don had a direct satellite radio contact from the plane to his 50,000-watt Christian station. He could give moment-by-moment updates on the ice conditions as we flew. Many times we had to warn people of rapidly rising water and impending floods. Sometimes, the villages would be engulfed by several feet of water, and huge ice flows would destroy houses and other property.

Since Don and I were both members of the Civil Air Patrol, which is an auxiliary of the U.S. Air Force, I would sometimes use the CAP Skyhawks to fly these missions instead of my plane. Also, since Fort Yukon was right in the middle of the north-bound airways, CAP had a nice new airplane hangar and Skyhawk plane available at all times for emergencies. Such emergencies would often arise due to lost or missing persons and downed airplanes. I flew many search and rescue missions out of Fort Yukon.

Rescue Mission

Around midnight on Christmas Eve, 1985, I got a phone call from the Anchorage CAP Wing Commander to fly a night search mission over the White Mountains to look for a downed plane. They thought they had a satellite fix on the plane's location. So, I took two CAP members and took off in the night with the Skyhawk. Shortly after takeoff, I began to get a signal from the downed aircraft's locator beacon. But since the area is so mountainous, the signal was bouncing around off the mountain walls. So, I took note of where the outside edges of the signals were, then measured to the center of the signal, and, sure enough, in the moonlight we could see a plane on a frozen lake between the mountain peaks. I dove down between the canyon walls and swooped low over the plane. We could see people outside the plane jumping and waving. It must have been minus 40 degrees.

Soon my radio crackled to life on the emergency frequency. The pilot, using a battery-powered hand transmitter, said everyone was okay, but they were very cold and hungry. So, we flew back over them and dropped blankets, food, and other supplies. I told them that we would send a helicopter at first light in the morning to rescue them. That search ended well; praise the Lord!

Troubling Encounter

During the winter months, I would start the wood stove fires in the Fort Yukon church at about 5:00 a.m. on Sunday morning. I got a fire going first in the fellowship hall where Sunday School was held for the kids; then I would start a fire in the large, double 55-gallon barrel stove. That big stove really put out the heat. I would turn on a large fan to circulate the heat in the church. Even with minus 50-degree temperatures outside, the church would be cozy by 10:00 a.m. I would then just keep the fires burning low during the day till evening service at 7:00.

One Saturday night, Carol and I went to the village laundromat since our washer wasn't working at the time. While waiting for the clothes to finish, a young man, obviously intoxicated, came in and confronted me. He was very aggressive and angry. I tried to calm him and told him that Jesus loved him and had the answer to his need. He just screamed at me, "I don't need Jesus! I don't need anybody!" Then he took a wild swing at my face. I quickly turned and leaned back, but his fist caught me square on my neck, knocking me backward against the wall. He rapidly ran out the door and down the street a short distance, and suddenly dropped dead!

I was stunned by what had just happened. Why did that young man have to die like that and go into eternity without God? How I wish I could have had more of an opportunity to minister to him so he could have understood how much God loved him. Yet, the realization came that Satan is a destroyer and he will destroy as many lives as he can.

Special Visitors

During the summer, we had the joy of having Pastor Orville and Sylvia Scantlin come from our home church in Lake Fork, Idaho, to hold a kid's crusade in four of our villages. Sylvia was an amazing lady, wonderful storyteller, and had God-given wisdom in knowing how to handle even unruly children. I flew them down to Stevens village first; and they just loved it, and the people loved them. An added blessing, Sylvia cooked with salmon fish oil which made the food taste great!

The next week, I flew the Scantlin's to Beaver village for a week. Things got interesting, however, after a native hunter shot a small bear cub and dragged it into the village. The mother bear came into the village looking for her cub and literally terrorized the village, including the Scantlin's, for two days! The Scantlin's couldn't leave the parsonage without danger of being attacked. The thick underbrush nearby allowed the bear to hide and attack at will. Finally, one of the hunters shot the mother bear and the Scantlin's were able to do a three-day crusade.

From Beaver, I flew them to Chalkytsik. Every village was greatly blessed by their ministry. Then, at Fort Yukon, Sylvia had 100 kids at the crusade. With help from our church women, many of the children really got to know Jesus. The kids were so proud of all the things they made at VBS. The Scantlin's worked hard, holding VBS during the day and services for adults at night.

After the Scantlin's left, I took a walk along the slough behind the Alaska Commercial store where I worked. As I walked, I noticed something unusual floating in the water. I bent down and looked more closely, and it appeared to be a body! I ran to the police station and got an officer who confirmed it was a dead man. By then, many in the village had gathered as we pulled the body out of the water. Apparently, the man had been intoxicated and stumbled into the water and drowned. It is so sad to see anyone leave this world without Jesus. Carol and I consoled the family and assisted with the funeral as well at the Episcopal church.

A Disturbing Call

Not long afterward, I received a phone call from my brother Art. He was very upset and sobbed as he told me about a dream he just had. "Rick, please don't fly your plane anymore!" he said, "I just dreamed that you and Carol were flying over some really tall, rocky, snow-capped mountains in a storm, when suddenly your plane burst into flames and went down! Please don't fly that plane anymore!"

I took Art's plea seriously, as he had called me before telling of dreams that had come to pass. But after gathering my thoughts and remembering our call, I spoke what came to my spirit.

"Art, God called Carol and me to do this ministry even though it does involve danger. We know the risks, and that we truly might die in an airplane crash doing our ministry. We have accepted that risk. I believe that God gave you that dream so that you may pray for God's protection over us. I cannot quit doing what God has called us to do. God can turn this dream into a real blessing if He sends His angels again to protect us. If we die, you will know where to find us in eternity."

Less than a week later, Carol and I were flying from Fairbanks to Fort Yukon over the White Mountain range with low visibility and turbulence. Suddenly, there was an overwhelming smell of gas in the cockpit. Carol pointed and screamed out, "Rick! Look, there is gas spraying out from under the instrument panel!"

How could that be? I wondered. There was no pressurized gas line under the instrument panel. I frantically tried to locate where the gas was spurting out from, but could not. Then, as I looked out at the snow-capped, rocky peaks below us, I remembered Art's call only a week before.

After a few moments, I spotted a large hole in the clouds over a small river. I immediately put the plane into a steep, slipping spiral through the hole, thinking I could possibly land in the river and we could make it to the beach. The steep mountain rock walls were close by as we spiraled down.

Amazingly, when we descended close to the river, the turbulence quit, as did the spurting gas. I opened the vents and windows and asked Carol, "Shall we try for Fort Yukon 60 miles away, or shall I land in the river?"

"Try for Fort Yukon," she said. So that's what we did, and we made it just fine. After landing, I crawled under the instrument panel and saw where the gas was spewing from. While working on the radios or something else behind the panel, the mechanic had accidentally kinked the primer fuel line. When we encountered turbulence over the mountains, the gas sloshing in the fuel tanks created enough pressure to cause the line to break at the bend. There is no doubt that God was with us in the plane and saved our lives again. Praise the Lord!

A Special Visit

Carol's parents, Ted and Mary Maenpa, flew up from Idaho and visited for 10 days. It was so nice to have them with us again. They had visited previously in Wainwright and Shaktoolik. We flew them down to Stevens and to Beaver villages for services with us. Ted played his harmonica for the people and gave testimonies. Also, while they were with us, we went fishing in our flat-bottomed river boat and caught some nice salmon. We invited our congregation to come to an outdoor picnic under the trees and enjoyed barbequed salmon. Mary canned the rest of the salmon to take home when they left.

Dwight's Medical Emergency

One day, early in December 1985, our son Dwight asked to go alone to Fairbanks on a Christmas shopping trip. He was 17 years old and had worked regularly at the Alaska Commercial store as a stocker. He had earned a little money, and since he had never flown alone anywhere before, he wanted to test his wings.

Dwight got his ticket on Harold's Air Service and left on the early morning flight to Fairbanks. We told him to call us when he got there, which he did. He was going to get a taxi from the airport to downtown, shop through the day, and stay at a reasonable hotel for the night. Then he would fly home the next morning.

All was well until the next morning. When we drove to the airstrip to meet the plane, it didn't arrive. So, we called the airlines and were told that the plane needed some repair which was underway, and that Dwight would arrive on the noon flight. We also were told that Dwight had arrived for the early flight, checked his bags, and then left till the later flight.

A few minutes before noon, we drove to the airport again to meet Dwight's flight. The plane landed, but Dwight was nowhere to be seen. In a near panic, we rushed home and called the airline in Fairbanks again. We learned that Dwight's bags were still there, but he hadn't show up for the flight. We called pastors, hospitals, even the jail. No one had seen Dwight. I called the police to see what they could do and was told that Dwight hadn't been missing long enough to launch a search. Carol and I prayed and also called our congregation, and pastors in Fairbanks, as well as the district office. All of them went to prayer.

Carol and I began to prepare our plane for a flight to Fairbanks, but, upon checking the weather, we learned that a severe Arctic storm was moving in. So, we caught the next commercial flight out of Fort Yukon that evening. The weather got so bad before we landed at Fairbanks that, after attempting two landings without success, the pilot got on the intercom and said, "I will try one more time to get down; if we cannot, we will have to go to

Anchorage." Carol and I buried our heads in our hands and prayed, "Please, Lord, let us land!" Thank God, the pilot made it down!

A dear Christian brother handed us the keys to his four-wheel-drive SUV and said, "Use it till you find your son." Amazingly, we ran across one of our new police officers from Fort Yukon. He was also stuck in Fairbanks due to the weather. He told us, "I will jump on this right now! I know lots of people here in Fairbanks. If Dwight is here, we'll find him."

We all searched, made calls, and prayed. Finally, around 11:00 p.m., the officer called our room and said, "I found Dwight. He is in the emergency room at the hospital. Dwight had stumbled into an urgent care clinic and was rushed to the emergency room for an immediate appendectomy. He is in the recovery room and is going to be fine."

Praise God, what a relief! Earlier, the officer had told us that some youth recently had disappeared, and foul play was suspected. So, it was wonderful to hear that Dwight was okay. When we inquired as to why the hospital hadn't called us, we were told that Dwight was in such bad condition when they got him, he was rushed straight to emergency surgery. The moment the surgeon touched Dwight's appendix, it burst in his abdomen. Thankfully, they were able to clean his abdominal cavity well. The hospital had tried to call us at Fort Yukon, but we were gone from the house and did not have an answering machine.

When we got to the hospital after midnight, Dwight was still groggy and quite sick as he came out of anesthesia. We hugged him tight and also thanked the officer heartily for his help. Carol and I then went back to the apartment at First Assembly and slept the night. Dwight was released to us the next day. He was very sore and walked slowly. After another day in Fairbanks, we flew back to Fort Yukon. Dwight recovered well from his experience, though he tried hard not to laugh, cough, or sneeze for several days as it hurt too badly!

Superintendent Tours

Our district superintendent Jack Bransford loved to fly out to Fort Yukon to be in services with us. At one point, he flew out during a very cold spell in the interior of Alaska to make our Yukon River circuit to Stevens and Beaver villages. Preparing to fly in these temperatures was quite a process. I warmed the plane engine with the catalytic heater, took off the bright orange wing and windshield covers, put an eight-ounce bottle of denatured alcohol in each fuel tank to dissolve all floating frost in the fuel, set all the engine controls and set the brakes. Then I hand-propped the engine to start it, as it was too cold for the battery to crank the engine.

After the engine started and idled smoothly, Carol climbed into the back seat, and Jack sat beside me.

We slowly taxied out to the runway to let all temperatures stabilize, and to check all instruments and controls. I announced on the radio our takeoff and direction of flight to the flight service. We were ready to fly.

We were just starting our climb-out at about 100 feet over the trees when the engine suddenly sputtered badly and lost almost all power. As we rapidly descended toward the trees, I caught sight of the fuel pressure gauge which was showing nearly zero! Instinctively, I switched fuel tanks to the right-tip tank, hit the boost pump, cross-controlled the rudder and ailerons, and got the right wing up higher than the engine so the fuel would gravity feed into the engine. It worked! The engine roared back to full power just before we hit the trees, and we climbed out. Oh, the joys and challenges of flying in Alaska!

I had encountered this kind of situation before. The fuel would get so cold in the wings and the fuel pump diaphragm would become too stiff to keep up with the full-power fuel flow needed for takeoff. So, from that point on, I always had a finger on the boost pump during takeoff and climb-out.

After landing at Stevens village, we got the fire going and had the evening service in the parsonage. What a powerful service! The joy of the Lord was so real. We enjoyed anointed singing and testimonies; and Brother Bransford's ministry of the Word was tremendous. His message was followed by a powerful time of prayer.

Just before going to bed, Brother Bransford and I went to the airplane to get the catalytic engine heater going. Then I put on the engine cowl and tightly secured the engine cover.

It must have dropped to minus 50 degrees before morning. Brother Bransford slept on the lower bunk and kept getting cold, so he would get up and stoke the fire. On the upper bunk, Carol and I were near the ceiling and nearly roasted! But morning came cold and clear. After breakfast, we took off for Beaver.

We landed at Beaver and put the engine cover on the plane which would keep the engine warm for about eight hours, if there was little or no wind. By early afternoon, the parsonage was warm enough to have service. Then we took off for Fort Yukon before it got dark, as there were no runway lights at Beaver. Jack stayed over for our Sunday services at Fort Yukon and left for Anchorage on Monday.

Overcoming Challenges of Change

As pastor, I encountered a time when the Fort Yukon church board and I were working on some significant changes, but it seemed we could not come to agreement on how to accomplish the changes. During my study and prayer time, I felt compelled of the Holy Spirit to call a special meeting of the board. So, I sent out an urgent letter to all the board members to meet at a specific time at the church office. When the board members arrived, they were somewhat upset that I had called an urgent meeting. I told them, "The urgent thing is that God has called us to prayer together until we hear from heaven. We are so far apart on what to do that we have allowed our own feelings to enter into what God wants to do. So, Brethren, I am calling us to prayer now so that we can get our hearts in tune with God."

God came down! We wept, we repented, we cried out for God's perfect will, and we hugged each other. Then we laid the problems on the table and voted with a hundred percent voting in favor of the proposed changes. We all laughed and praised God together as we realized that God had once again done a miracle of healing in our body of believers.

When people of God are in tune with God, the church will run like a well-oiled machine. All the hills and valleys that we may encounter only become minor bumps in the road of life. After this breakthrough, it was such a joy to see people that had been very hostile to the gospel get saved and filled with the Holy Spirit, both in Fort Yukon and in other villages as well. To God be the glory!

Law Enforcement and Rescue Patrols

On occasion, I was called upon to fly some rather unusual missions. One such mission happened on a very cold day with low visibility and an icy fog. A local Alaska state trooper came by the parsonage and asked me to take him on a secret and unexpected flight over an area where poachers were suspected of killing moose. An informant had alerted him as to where they were camping, and he wanted to check it out from a plane that was not marked with law enforcement insignia. So, we drove quickly to the airport and took off.

The trooper gave me a coordinate to fly at very low altitude, approaching the camp from a different direction. Visibility was a mile or less, so we came upon the poachers unexpectedly. After the flyover, the officer never divulged to me what he had seen or what actions were taken, but the poaching problem ceased in that area.

That same spring, in May, I was notified by the Civil Air Patrol commander that a Cessna 185 on skis was missing somewhere north of the Yukon River not far from Stevens village. So, the commander and I got in a CAP Skyhawk and we took off toward the village. Soon after takeoff we picked up a signal from an emergency locator beacon. As we flew over, we saw four men on the ice, waving at us. The Cessna's wheel skis had broken through the ice, and the nose of the plane was under water. But the wings were on top of the ice holding the plane from falling through.

Using a handheld radio, the pilot reported that they were all okay, but were wet and cold and wanted us to land and pick them up. I replied, "You are on skis and broke through the ice; if I try to land on that thin ice with wheels, we'll have two wrecked planes to rescue" So, I told him that I would climb to 6,000 feet, notify Fairbanks control of the coordinates where we had found them, and request that they send a helicopter right away.

"I will drop you some food and blankets to tide you over till you are rescued," I added. So, we flew low over them and dropped the supplies. Before the day was over, they were picked up by a helicopter and flown to Fairbanks. Afterward, a large Skycrane helicopter was sent to lift the plane out of the water with a strap cradle and transport it back to Fairbanks.

Ministry Transition

By 1986, our four-year missionary term at Fort Yukon was coming to an end and it seemed there were still so many loose ends to pull together. One of those would be finding a pastor to take our place. Soon, however, I got a call from a native pastor who also was a missionary appointed by Assemblies of God U.S. Missions. He told me that he had been feeling a real burden for Fort Yukon and was interested in coming when we left. I was so excited that I shouted praise to the Lord! He wasn't an airplane pilot, but he certainly would be able to relate to the culture of the Athabaskan people.

We flew our last few village circuits and said our goodbyes, hugged necks, and wept with the village people; they didn't want to see us go. Afterward, we had a moving sale and sold our pickup, snowmobiles, and three-wheeler Honda. A school teacher at Fort Yukon purchased our airplane.

Dwight had already flown to Idaho and was staying with Carol's parents in Lake Fork. We proceeded to pack several 60-pound boxes and mailed them to Idaho.

The new missionary came two days before we left, so we had opportunity to orient him and his wife to the mission and introduce them to the villagers. After holding our last service at Fort Yukon and saying goodbye to our congregation, we handed the keys to the new missionary couple and boarded a plane to Fairbanks. From there we would head to Idaho for itineration.

Upon landing, we transferred our luggage to a nice, 1977 Ford Landau four-door sedan that we had already purchased and headed down the Alaska Highway once again for Idaho. The trip took five days, but it was the most comfortable trip we had ever made down the Highway. The old Ford ran well, but it used about a quart of oil with every tank of gas. It wasn't leaking oil, it was burning oil. However, we got 13-plus miles per gallon. Before then, nine miles per gallon was the best mileage we had ever achieved with our pickup and camper/trailer combo.

After arriving in Idaho, we evaluated the problem

with the car engine and decided to put in a remanufactured long-block 400M engine. We also had the car repainted, and it came out beautifully. Both the paint job and the engine were done at a reasonable price. We hooked my parent's 12-foot camp trailer to our Ford and began our itinerary. It pulled the trailer just fine.

We had set up our itinerary to visit churches throughout the Southern Idaho District. We enjoyed the itinerary, but the call of God to get back to the mission field was always strong in our hearts. It was strange to us not to have an airplane during this time; it seemed to take so long to get anywhere!

During our itinerary, our remanufactured engine began to break valve springs and drop the valve on top of the piston which really started tearing things up in the engine. Then it dawned on me why the engine was doing that. Before I installed the engine, I knew we were going to be towing a trailer most of the time. So, I pulled out the stock camshaft and installed a Crane 260 RV cam to give the engine more low-end and mid-range torque and better gas mileage. That part of the cam did well. However, when I installed the hydraulic lifters, I had primed the lifters (filled) them with oil. On some older versions of engines, that was the norm. But not on this engine's type of lifters. So, when I cranked up the engine, I wondered why it snorted, popped, and backfired through the carburetor several times. The lifters were opening the valves so far that the valve springs were bottoming out and being bound and weakened. One by one, they began to fail with possibly catastrophic results.

When a spring broke, it really hampered our itinerary schedule, as the car became totally unreliable. The valve springs just kept failing. Thankfully, in God's good providence, a car dealer in Nampa loved the car despite its problems and offered us $4,000 for it on trade for a nice heavy-duty 1987 pickup. That ended our troubles. We had come to learn that whenever we ministered to the needs of people or church, God took care of us.

Expanded District Itineraries

After finishing our itinerary in Idaho, we traveled to the Wyoming District Council where Ivar Frick, superintendent of the Michigan District, was the key speaker. During an opening in an afternoon session, I was asked to speak briefly about our missionary work in Alaska. Superintendent Frick was so moved by what God gave me to say that he pulled me aside and said, "Brother Rick, God spoke to me while you were speaking. I am to invite you to come to the Michigan District to raise your support. Though I have not done this in 20 years, I am supposed to set up your itinerary. Just give me three to four months to get it set up." Carol and I were speechless! Truly God was blessing us. So, after we itinerated through the Wyoming District, we set our sights for Michigan. In August 1987, we drove our pickup and trailer to Michigan and began our itinerary.

Our first service was at Fair Haven Assembly of God in Dearborn Heights. The pastor there invited us to camp in the church parking lot and base from there during most of our time in Michigan. Initially, thirteen churches had scheduled us to come, but as soon as we began having services, we started to receive calls from other churches, enough to fill the winter of 1987-88. What a winter it was! Despite heavy snow at times, it became clear to Carol and me that God had ordained our coming to Michigan. We were so blessed by a powerful anointing of the Holy Spirit in our services. Along the way, God sent us to some troubled churches with a message of healing and reconciliation.

As our itinerary drew to a close in the Lower 48, it was time to pack up our gear and head back to Alaska. However, during our itinerary, a change of leadership took place in the Alaska District, and we were now requested to move to Emmonak village on the Yukon Delta, about 22 miles from the Bering Sea. We also would be ministering to several other villages close by. We learned that the former missionary would be leaving some very useful Speed the Light equipment including a 20-foot, flat-bottomed boat with a 40-horsepower Mercury outboard motor. This would prove to be a blessing to our ministry there.

Emmonak

Emmonak is 600 miles west of Anchorage, and just as far from the closest road. The only way into the village is by air or by supply barges that come down the Yukon River from Tanana close to Fairbanks. Since we would be in such a remote area, we sold our 21-foot RV trailer and boxed up all our belongings and mailed them to Emmonak. We also crated Dwight's four-wheel Yamaha 350 into the back of our pickup, along with other larger items.

We said our goodbyes once again and headed back up the Alaska Highway. Our truck was nice to travel in, and, thankfully, the Highway was paved much of the way by this time. We certainly didn't miss navigating 1,200 miles of dirt road and potholes! Most of the 10 percent grade hills also were gone, so the trip went pretty well. However, gas and other supplies along the Highway were almost double Idaho prices, so we were thankful for the generosity of God's people during our itinerary.

After five days of travel, we arrived in Fairbanks. We unloaded Dwight's four-wheeler at the barge landing in Tanana for shipping to Emmonak. Then we drove some 400 miles to Anchorage to make final plans at the Alaska District office and get other needed supplies sent out to the village.

Mike Herr, pastor at Anchorage Crossroads Assembly of God, who also had been a car dealer, sold our Ford pickup for us. He also took us to the airport where we boarded a 737 jet and flew to Saint Mary's. This was an interesting experience as the St. Mary's airport is a gravel airstrip on top of a mountain. With a loud roar along with flying gravel and dust, the 737 touched down. There we changed to a little 207 Cessna single-engine plane for the final 75 miles to Emmonak. In Emmonak, we were picked up by a village delivery truck as there was more freight than passengers.

Emmonak has been called "Mud City USA." Was this ever right! The Yukon Delta is muddy from sediment coming all the way from Canada and coursing through Alaska. We rarely left the house without rubber boots on. Frequent summer rains in the delta turned the village into a mud bog.

The government had directed numerous barge-loads of rock and gravel to be hauled down from Mountain Village about 60 miles up the Yukon River. It was used to build a few roads through the village; probably two or three miles of road altogether. The rock and gravel also were used to build a nice 5,000-foot runway at the airport.

The two-story mission in Emmonak was very nice. A 40- by 60-foot parsonage was positioned upstairs with the church downstairs. The church seated 60 people nicely. The building was heated by oil and hot water radiators, which worked well, but were very expensive to operate, so we used driftwood as much as possible to heat the parsonage. We collected the wood with our big flat-bottomed boat or with the snowmobile and sled in the winter.

Not long after we arrived, we requested that a team of MAPS workers come out to help us level the building. It was built up about four feet off the ground and sat on 12 huge, treated 4- by 12-foot crisscrossed pads. The building had to be raised above the ground since almost every spring some two to three feet of flood water came into the village when ice jammed the river during the spring breakup. The pads just sat on top of the mud which would heave and settle, jamming doors and warping the floors. They had to be leveled. Getting that done by the MAPS team was a tremendous help!

Emmonak is inhabited by Yupik Eskimos. As with ministering to people in other villages, we had to earn their respect. We had to prove that we really loved them. Early on, we faced some tests from a few agnostic people, but we just loved them in spite of their responses. Soon they became friendly as they realized we really cared.

After we got settled in, Carol, Dwight, and I took a National Weather Service training course. The previous missionary had done weather reporting from the parsonage, so the Weather Service wanted to keep the weather equipment there. Reporting required sending up weather balloons and calling in the data hourly to Bethel Flight Service Station, 10 hours per day. Dwight did most of the reporting, but Carol and I would relieve him when we were not out on ministry trips.

Village Ministries

During the milder weather, we traveled from village to village with the flat-bottomed river boat. We held regular services in Alakanuk village since they had no pastor. Alakanuk was about 20 miles down the Yukon River. We had awesome services there.

We also visited Kotlik village by boat; a village situated some 40 miles northeast of us, up the sloughs. As winter arrived and the river froze, we traveled over snow trails and river ice by snow machine and sled. The winters there were very snowy and windy, but not quite as severe as other places had been. However, the temperatures were always below zero, usually around minus 10 to 25, with dips to minus 30 or 40.

By spring, we were very anxious to get another airplane. Full Gospel Assembly of God in Westland, Michigan, invited me to fly in and speak at their missions convention and raise money for our much-needed plane. We surely had wonderful services with them. There was a sweet and powerful move of the Holy Spirit in the services.

An "Old Friend" Returns

When I returned to Emmonak, I received a phone call from the school teacher named Bonnie, to whom we had sold our Cherokee 140 airplane two years before. She had recently flown the plane to Fairbanks for an annual inspection and learned that the engine was eating itself on the inside. It was a miracle that she arrived in Fairbanks without a failure. She offered to sell it back to me for $5,000 with the blown engine. After estimating the cost to totally remanufacture the engine, I figured that the Cherokee plane still was just what we wanted for now. So, with the $5,000 that Full Gospel Assembly gave us, we bought the plane. Several other churches and individuals covered the expense of the remanufactured engine, so, when it was completed, I flew to Fairbanks and brought the plane home.

How happy we were! We had always loved that little plane. One great advantage was that it could use auto fuel instead of the more expensive aviation fuel. Although a lot of controversy surrounded the use of auto fuel in an airplane, I flew hundreds of hours with it. When my mechanic examined the engine, he said, "That is the cleanest airplane engine I have ever seen!"

As in previous mission stations, I again became very involved in search and rescue flying as well as medical evacuations. I flew coordinated search and rescue flights with the Coast Guard, Civil Air Patrol, and the Department of Public Safety. We also flew countless flights to villages for MAPS building projects as well as missionary and evangelistic services across Alaska.

Draught of Fish

During our time in Emmonak, I became well acquainted with Missionary John Covlasky and his two sons. They each had fishing boats and came to Emmonak and to Alukanuk every summer for salmon gill net fishing. John had a real burden to establish an Assemblies of God mission at Sheldon's Point. So, he asked me if I'd be willing to man the net on his boat during the short month of salmon season. He wanted to raise enough money to pay for the new mission building.

We also had with us Kevin Priest, an 18-year-old Christian young man from Oil City, Michigan, with whom Carol and I became acquainted during our Michigan itinerary. Earlier, Kevin had a real burden to fly up on a MAPS project to assist Carol and me with painting and working on our mission in Emmonak. He also helped us get firewood for the mission. After that trip, Kevin wanted to come back and help on the boat during the fishing season. We surely enjoyed having him around.

On the very first day of fishing season, the Fish and Game Department announced there would not be many fish that year, which was discouraging. So, a few minutes before we dropped our 300-foot net into the water, I said, "John, Kevin, lets join hands and pray for a miracle of fish." While we prayed, God came down and we began to weep before the Lord and worship Him, raising our clasped hands heavenward. Suddenly, I heard a splashing sound and looked at the water. All around us king salmon were on the surface so close together they were touching each other!

At that point, it was time to drop the net into the water. Moments after doing so the net began to sink. When John tried to winch it in, it was so full of fish we couldn't raise the net! John got so excited and then became very concerned as he feared we would be taken downstream and into the rapids and lose everything.

"Cut loose the net lest we lose it all!" he said.

"John, no!" I cried out. "God has given us this tremendous net of fish worth thousands of dollars. Put the boat into gear at low idle and angle it toward the sloped beach about a mile away; I believe we can make it."

John put the boat into gear and we were soon pulling that big load of fish onto the beach. We shouted, praised the Lord, and danced before the Lord! The boat was so full of fish we nearly swamped it. That first net brought over $6,000 toward the mission! We couldn't help but recall the story about Peter and the great draught of fish in

Luke 5:1-11. That miracle happened again!

Snagged!

On one occasion, Kevin and I took a boat trip in an old junk boat on which I had installed a makeshift plywood mount for a 25-horsepower outboard motor. We were going full speed across the Yukon River when we ran right over a Fish and Game Department fish test net that I didn't know was there. Wham! The force of the prop snagging and tangling up in the heavy net stopped us so quickly that both of us nearly flew out of the boat.

The force also damaged the keel and water began pouring into the boat. We were so tangled up in the net that it took me some 15 to 20 minutes to cut and pry the boat loose from the net. Kevin bailed water out of the boat with a bucket until I freed the boat from the net. Once we started moving, the water stopped pouring in and we were able to get back to Emmonak just fine, thank the Lord!

Mission Building Adventures

Kevin also helped us with supplies from the barge that came in from Nenana down the Yukon River to Sheldon's Point, carrying materials for the new Assemblies of God mission there. We loaded our Speed the Light four-wheel Foreman Honda onto John Cavlasky's big boat along with my trailer that I towed behind the Honda. We would use the four-wheeler and trailer to haul the lumber and other materials from the barge landing site.

This turned out to be quite a job, but it went well. However, the barge was delayed a few days due to low water. Because of the delay, Kevin was not able to stay to finish the building and had to return to Emmonak. So, William, a young native man from Emmonak who had come down to help us, joined Kevin and me in my little 18-foot cabin boat and we headed back up the Yukon River to Emmonak, about a 40-mile trip.

On our way, the weather began to deteriorate rapidly with wind gusting to nearly 40 miles per hour. My little boat did well on the waves until we got to the Kwiguk slough that would take us from the Yukon River to Emmonak. As we navigated around the bend toward the village, the waves rose to some 12 to 15 feet. We were taking on water and we began to wonder if we would make it. We prayed and just kept going. It was impossible to beach along the sheer wall banks. Soon, however, we were anchored in Emmonak, shaken up and a bit seasick, but alive!

As we loaded Kevin's luggage in our plane the next morning, the weather forecast to Anchorage was good. Carol got in the back seat and Kevin sat beside me. We prayed again for God's protection and blessing and took off for the McGrath fuel and rest stop half way to Anchorage. After our fuel stop, we climbed to 10,000 feet over Rainy Pass in the Alaska Range, as there were strong winds and turbulence at lower altitudes. The view was beautiful with Mr. McKinley in all its majesty off to the left. We could see numerous glaciers as well.

As we approached Merrill Field airport in Anchorage, one of the busiest airports in the world, my radio gave out right after I got my coordinates and clearances for landing. I would have to make my landing on light signals from the control tower, and I was very concerned. However, as we made our landing approach, all went well. We taxied our plane to the aircraft radio shop and left the plane there. Then we rented a car, drove around Anchorage for a while, and stayed overnight with our U.S. Missions Coordinator, James P. Schulz and his wife.

After taking Kevin to the airport for his flight back to Michigan, Carol and I picked up some needed supplies and flew back to Emmonak. I was able to get back to Sheldon's Point just in time to help the crew put up the building. It turned out to be a really nice little mission station, measuring 20- by 24 feet with an 8- by 8-foot porch. The building was heated with a pot oil heater. After the mission was completed, we had our first service. The little mission was filled with precious Native people worshiping the Lord together. Sheldon's Point had only about 100 residents at that time, and the only other church was a small Catholic mission.

As weather allowed, Carol and I traveled to Sheldon's Point weekly by boat, snowmobile, or plane. There were no runway lights, so, during the dark winter season, we would fly down at the crack of dawn, get the heat going in the church's oil heater, then walk around the village and visit the people and invite them to the service that night. After the service, we would eat power bars and other simple snacks, heat the plane engine with a pot heater or catalytic heater, and fly back to Emmonak after daybreak which was very short.

During this time, a new Native couple, Sonny Joseph and his family had moved to Alukanuk village as interim pastors at the Assembly of God mission there. They were in training with the Far North Bible School and I was their mentor. We went many times with Sonny to have services at Sheldon's Point as we knew our term would extend only two more years, and we wanted to get him established in the work there. Sonny would go down by boat in summer and snowmobile in the winter.

Crisis on the Ice

Shortly after the freeze-up of the Yukon River, when the ice was still only some two to three inches thick, the natives would be anxious to make snowmobile trails on the river to the adjoining villages. Carol and I always took advantage of those winter trails as they were quite smooth, and we could make good time on a fast snowmobile.

One time, when Carol and I needed to go to

Alukanuk village for a service, our snowmobile was needing repair. So, we used Dwight's Polaris 650, 3-cylinder, Indy snowmobile that had over 90 horsepower. The trip down went well. We had a wonderful service and prayer time together with the Alukanuk people.

After the service, it was dark, and it had started snowing and blowing some. However, Carol and I fastened our supplies and headed back for Emmonak. All went well until we turned onto the wide part of the Yukon River about five miles out of Emmonak. The wind had really picked up and the snow was restricting visibility. However, I could still see the airport beacon clearly through the storm, so we kept going.

At one point, I noticed that I had gotten off the trail and I knew there was the possibility of open water around the main channel. However, I didn't know which side of the trail we were on. As we moved swiftly along at about 40 miles per hour, suddenly, right in front of us, I saw open water! We were too close to stop or turn, and I knew that the river channel was some 90 to 120 feet deep and fairly swift. So, I shouted, "Jesus, help us!" and held the throttle wide open.

Carol grabbed me tightly around the waist, screaming out to Jesus as well. We hit the water at full speed. Water flew up in our faces, but it felt like the snowmobile was actually gaining speed on top of the water! After what seemed like forever on open water, there was a hard "clang" when we hit the opposite side of the giant hole and were back on the ice. We must have been going 80 miles per hour or more skimming over the open water!

I kept the speed up for fear of encountering more open water, keeping an eye on the airport beacon. Finally, we came upon the trail and I slowed down and stopped. Carol and I were both soaking wet and shaking from the cold and from the exhilaration of what had just happened. Had I tried to stop, we would have gone down into the river and been taken under the ice by the strong current. Also, had we been riding our lower-powered snowmobile instead of Dwight's, we would not have skimmed over the water. Truly, the Lord had sent His angels again to protect us!

Caterpillar on the Ice

The village council knew of my experience with operating heavy equipment. So, after the Yukon River froze to a depth of three to four feet, they asked me if I would build an ice road to the nearby villages. I was not sure about this. Was I really ready to take a 50,000-pound Caterpillar earth mover with a giant snow blade out on the river that had nearly claimed our lives? A Caterpillar had not broken through the ice in Emmonak; however, two or more had been lost over the years near other villages. Each time, the drivers were not found. I talked this over with Carol and prayed about it. Afterward, despite the risks, I felt a peace in my heart to bless the villagers in this manner.

What little hair I have on top of my head still stands up when I think about this challenge. Initially, I used a large road grader to clear a path through about two miles of sloughs. I felt safer using the grader as it was on rubber tires and its long span would distribute its weight more evenly than the Cat. However, when I got out on the big, open Yukon River, the snow was too deep for the grader's center blade. So, I mounted the big Cat to do the rest of the road. I had to plow snow ramps for cars and trucks to get on and off the river. With God's help and protection, the road was completed. It was wonderful to have the ice road for several months during the winter.

Search for Lost Boaters

Sometime after completing the ice road project, I received a phone call from the village council asking if I would fly a search and rescue mission for some missing local people. They had left their fish camp by boat in a strong wind storm in an attempt to get to Emmonak via the south fork of the Yukon River. So, I took three spotters with me and took off in our Cherokee and flew the route to their fish camp. We flew back and forth, each time moving farther out over the water. We became very concerned as at that time the wind was blowing some 30-plus miles per hour from the Siberian side of the Norton Sound. Loose ice had piled up for miles out to sea. We flew for several hours till our fuel was nearly exhausted, but to no avail. During the night, the wind changed to an east wind blowing off the delta toward Siberia and had increased to nearly 50 miles per hour.

In the morning, the weather report was not good. Not only was the wind very strong, there was heavy fog along with icing conditions. Despite these conditions, the U. S. Coast Guard was sending out a Hercules search plane with metal detectors and radar, and a Sikorsky Jolly Green Giant helicopter to search for the lost boaters. They asked me to fly a coordinated search grid with them as the ice around the point was breaking up and going out to sea. If the fishermen's boat was stuck on the ice, they would be taken out to sea and would no doubt perish.

So, I gathered my spotters again and we prayed for favor and protection in this search. We would be putting our own lives in great danger flying in these conditions. We took off and hugged the coast line for the first leg of the search. It was so turbulent that I had to fly sideways to keep lined up with the coast. We made it back to the fishermen's take-off point, turned around, and flew out over the ice according to the grid. The visibility was dropping quickly, and we began to ice up. Yet, I felt compelled of the Holy Spirit to fly one more time out over the ice about a mile out to sea. Fog was closing in and the icing was getting worse.

As I started to turn back for Emmonak, one of my

spotters shouted, "There's a dark moving object barely visible in the fog." I quickly turned back and, sure enough, I saw two men jumping and waving their dark blankets from their boat that was solidly stuck in the ice. Soon they would be swept out to sea.

I quickly radioed the helicopter and gave the coordinates. The pilot said, "That can't be, we just came from there, and there was nothing." I assured them that we had found the target and that they must come quickly. The helicopter was only about 10 miles south of us, so the rescuers were there in less than five minutes. We circled the boat until the helicopter arrived and lowered a rescue basket. All of us laughed, wept, and praised the Lord as we watched the men being lifted safely into the helicopter.

I asked the pilot to land at Emmonak which was about 25 miles away. Oh, the joy and tears as the helicopter landed with us following behind. We watched the wives and families of the lost men run into the arms of their loved ones. Hugs and kisses of gratitude came to us as well. The families were sure their men had been lost at sea, but, praise God, the lost were found!

After a couple of days, the storm quit and the men we had rescued asked if I would fly them out to find their boat. However, when we arrived over the spot where they were rescued, the boat was nowhere to be found. Apparently, it had blown out to sea.

Though the men were saddened about losing their boat, they were grateful to be alive, and they had quite a story to tell!

Gathering Wood

After getting repairs made on our Speed the Light snowmobile, we rode out to the delta to search for wood. We gathered a lot of our firewood from driftwood that came down river during the spring ice breakup. A lot of birch and alder trees would get lodged in the willows along the delta. I had a nice 12- by 4-foot heavy duty sled for hauling wood. Nothing was quite as comfortable during cold winter days than huddling up around a crackling wood fire in the parsonage stove.

Also, during the summer, we would go up and down the Yukon searching for large spruce driftwood trees. Occasionally, we would find some that were two to three feet in diameter. We would buck them into large blocks, load them into our boat, and haul them to our woodshed with our 4 X 4 pickup truck. It was always good to get the woodshed filled before winter set in.

The previous missionary also had built a nice plywood steam bath sauna that we heated with wood. Sometimes, some of the native folk would come over on Saturday nights for a sauna.

Prevalence of Suicide

During our last two years at Emmonak, several suicides occurred. Harsh conditions, long periods of darkness, alcoholism, and other factors contributed to many of these suicides which always were so hard for families to deal with. They wanted some assurance that their loved ones would be in heaven. All I could say was that God is a righteous judge. He is not like man, He judges righteously and justly. Though these times were very difficult, they provided opportunity to minister to people about being sure their hearts were right with God.

A Call Home for Christmas

As Christmas 1990 approached, Carol's father, Ted Maenpa, was in very poor health. Carols' mother Mary asked if we could fly home for Christmas. She was certain Dad would pass during our stay. So, we flew to Idaho via commercial airlines and spent two weeks there. Dad's health seemed to actually improve while we were there. We even took him out to a pancake house in McCall and to a favorite Mexican restaurant. He really enjoyed our stay. We could see, however, that his mind was failing fast.

Soon it was time to return to Alaska. Before we left, I approached Ted, weeping, and asked, "Could I hear you pray just one more time before we leave?" I will never forget that prayer. Somehow,

Ted reached down to the depths of his soul and prayed the most beautiful prayer I had ever heard him pray. He prayed with a clear mind, in tune with the Holy Spirit, with tears running down his cheeks.

After saying goodbye once again, we loaded our bags into the rental car and headed back down the Payette River canyon and drove a hundred miles to Star to visit my parents. The next morning, we drove early to the Boise airport to catch our plane. At that time, the airline tickets to Alaska were over $1,000 per person.

We arrived back in Emmonak late the same day, tired and weary of flying. It was good to get back into the groove of snowmobiling to the closer villages and flying our Cherokee with Christian native workers to other villages for services and visits.

Sonny Joseph and his family were doing very well ministering in Alakanuk. That surely took a big load off Carol and me, but we still made at least two trips a month down there to visit and be in service with them.

A new missionary in Unalakleet was building a new church using the plans and blueprints from our Emmonak mission. We made several flights to help get their mission up and operating. Being a three-hour round trip, it was a significant journey to make.

Quick Return to Idaho

On the last day of January 1991, we received a phone call that we had feared would come soon. Gordon Coler, pastor in McCall, Idaho, told us that Carol's dad was with the Lord. Less than a month had passed since we had been there for Christmas. This time, Carol and I flew to Anchorage, picked up Dwight who was staying in Anchorage and worked at McDonalds, and flew commercial airlines to Seattle, Washington. There, we rented a car and drove the 300-plus miles to Lake Fork, Idaho, for Ted's funeral.

Funeral preparations seemed unreal. Was this really happening? Even though we knew Ted's passing was inevitable, we weren't totally ready for it. Other family drove or flew in from various places. Then, on funeral day, we all drove to a little white Finnish church and cemetery. Many extended family members and friends that we had not seen in years were there. A positive aspect of funerals is that they draw the family together.

Pastor Coler preached a powerful message about Ted's faith in God and his prayer life. He related that Ted's wife Mary told of how Ted would awaken her many times during the night praying. There was such a peace in knowing without a doubt that he was with the Lord.

Following the funeral and burial service, we all gathered for dinner and a time to reflect. Afterward, we all did what we could to prepare Mary for living alone without her lifelong love. We knew it was going to be hard for her. It was very hard for us all to leave her and return back to our mission. Financially, it had been quite a strain as well as we had spent more than $6,000 on airline tickets and car rentals in the past two months. But, God would soon provide help in an unexpected way.

Wonderful Provision

After we returned, the general manager of the Emmonak Corporation came to the parsonage and asked me if I would consider being manager of the tank farm which was the gas, oil, stove oil, and propane storage area for fuel sales and deliveries. He said, "I know you are a missionary and are very busy and would be called away many times for pastoral duties. However, you would have at least two or three hired hands to assist you and take over while you're away on ministry trips." I accepted the job, and it worked out wonderfully. Soon all the expenses of the trips to Idaho were paid off! Praise the Lord! Also, the fringe benefit of this was that I got to minister to and pray with a lot of people I probably would never have met otherwise. I had opportunity to become friends with hundreds of native people. Again, we were reminded that God works in mysterious ways His wonders to perform!

As I began working with the fuel delivery truck at the Emmonak Corporation, I discovered that it was set up with a really slow, engine-driven, vacuum pump to deliver stove oil into the customer's tanks. It took nearly an hour to deliver 300 gallons of stove oil. So, I researched a better pump system and found one that would deliver about 25 gallons a minute or more. The manager was all for it, so I ordered the pump kit and installed it when it came. What a difference! Not only was the pump much faster, it was a lot quieter as well. The old vacuum pump clattered like a snare drum, waking up the neighbors and making dogs howl!

During the deliveries, people usually wanted me to step in for coffee. Many visits became ministry opportunities through counseling and prayer. So, this job was a real blessing in so many ways. Also, the manager was good to let me leave almost at the drop of a hat to fly rescue missions or do ministry trips.

Tragic Death

Great tragedy struck the village when a 14-year-old boy who had been drinking and doing some drugs wanted to get higher. Someone told him to sniff fumes from a gas can and he would get really high. Hours later, the boy was found dead with his nose in the top of a five-gallon gas can. The village recoiled at this death. Something had to be done about the crazy kinds of deaths that were happening among the youth. At funerals, such as for this young man, parents and other loved ones often wanted assurance that their loved one's soul was right with the Lord. Again, I would preach to the living to walk with the Lord. God is the righteous Judge and He will judge fairly. However, the Holy Scriptures are very plain about those who die in their sin.

Ice Jams and Fishing Season

Soon it was spring, and the Emmonak villagers began preparing for the river ice breakup that many times resulted in flooding with two to three feet of water. We pulled our boat to the parsonage and tied it to the stairway as the flood could sometimes last for hours or even days.

Occasionally, the ice jams would be dynamited to make the water level go down. However, that was never necessary during the years we were there, as the floods lasted only a few hours, thankfully.

John Covlaski, with whom we caught the great draught of fish at Fork Yukon, flew out to Emmonak with his family and then went on down to Alukanuk to get their boats ready for fishing season. John wanted me to help him build a cabin with 360-degree visibility on his new 30-foot fishing boat. He loved the little cabin I had built on my 18-foot Lund boat that had in-cabin controls and Lexan windows all around. It was very comfortable in wet, windy weather.

We finished the cabin on John's boat a few days before fishing season. He was so excited about that cabin which we constructed out of two-by-two lumber fastened together with stainless steel screws.

The cabin had a one-quarter-inch marine plywood exterior which we painted with white weatherproof paint. We also installed sliding, one-quarter-inch Lexan doors front and rear.

John had a 130-horsepower motor on the boat that propelled it along quite well. There was a large aluminum net drum powered by a small Honda single-cylinder, five-horsepower motor to run the winch that pulled the 300-foot net back into the boat full of fish. As fish were caught, two helpers pulled the fish from the net and dropped them into the bottom of the boat as John pulled the net in and wound it on a large winch. A large net guide that looked like huge aluminum horns was positioned on the nose of the boat to keep the net straight.

Between income from the short commercial fishing season, managing the tank farm, and my missions budget, we had sufficient funds to fly our plane and operate our boat and all the other equipment required to do ministry there.

Sectional Representation

During this time, I also was privileged to serve as an Alaska District Sectional Representative. As part of that responsibility, Carol and I flew to all the mission stations in our section which encompassed a huge territory. Some missions required a three or four-hour flight. Yet, it was always such a joy to visit those very remote areas and the missionaries who served. They had no airplanes and lived hundreds of miles from the closest access roads. As often as possible, we would fly to the villages, have services there, and feel the heartbeat of the missionaries for the ministries to which God had called them. We would stay overnight, enjoy fellowship, pray with the missionaries and try to be a blessing to them in any way we could to further the call of God upon their lives.

A Generous Offer

One day, a dear brother came over to the parsonage for a visit. As we had coffee and rolls, he said, "I've been thinking and praying about something that I want to share with you. I have inherited several acres of land about 15 miles up the Yukon in a slough. Would you go with me in your boat? I will guide you to it. I would like to give a large portion of that land to the church for summer camp meetings."

I was surprised, but readily agreed to do so.

We went to the boat dock and took off up river. The property was a very nice, pretty area, very accessible by boat or float plane. We walked the whole area and measured off the piece of land he wanted to give to the church. I saw the great possibilities and even envisioned a large tent for services; there also was space for numerous camp tents. Even buildings could be erected as needed.

We went back to Emmonak and immediately

contacted the district office about the offer. There was great interest about establishing a church camp in the Yukon Delta area. So, we got the ball rolling on the paperwork and legal matters.

Portland General Council

Shortly after the fishing season in August, 1991, Carol and I flew to the Lower 48 to attend the Assemblies of God General Council in Portland, Oregon. We flew into Portland a week before council, rented a car, and drove to Lake Fork, Idaho, to pick up Carol's mother Mary. She would attend General Council and then fly to Alaska with us for a couple of weeks in Emmonak.

We also visited my parents Art and Appy in Star and connected with as many of our relatives and friends that we could cram into that week. Then we drove to Portland where we met up with Carol's brother John Maempa, his son John who was working with him at Council, and the Vic Vaughn family, including Jim and his family from Australia. Wow! What a great reunion!

God moved powerfully by His Holy Spirit in the Council services, and our time together with family was so wonderful. We were disappointed to see Council and our family reunion come to an end; but, when all was over, we again said our goodbyes and went our different ways. Mary boarded the jet with us and we took off for Alaska. Our hearts ached for

Mary as she seemed sad and was quiet a lot during the trip to Emmonak. She spoke of how lonely it had been since her lifelong love, Ted, had passed just seven months before.

Mary's Visit

We changed jets at Anchorage and flew on to St. Marie's on a smaller jet. Mary was very surprised when we landed on St. Marie's mountaintop gravel runway. The noise of the gravel and all the dust startled her at first, then, we all had a good laugh. We changed planes there to a single-engine Cessna for our final 75-mile leg to Emmonak.

After landing in Emmonak, we threw all our bags into our Ford 4x4 pickup and bounced the last two miles to the parsonage. Very tired, we all crashed for good nap.

When Mary got up that first morning, she went to the large living room window in our parsonage, looked up to heaven, and began to thank the Lord aloud for one more day to serve Him, and for being one more day closer to seeing Him and her dear husband. Carol and I both broke into tears when we saw and heard Mom's prayer. She started each day with that same prayer. Then she would sit down with her Bible and begin to lovingly read God's Word as she sipped her first cup of coffee before breakfast.

After breakfast on Mary's first day, we climbed

into the pickup and drove around the village and took her to the village stores. There were two major stores, the Alaska Commercial and the Emmonak Corporation store. For lunch, we visited our one restaurant and had an "Alaska King Burger." We also introduced her to many of our native friends and church folk.

During the next few days, we flew Mary to Sheldon's Point village for church services; we also went to Alukanuk in our cabin boat. She was so blessed as she witnessed the native people being touched by the Holy Spirit.

One day, Mary got ambitious and made some wonderful Finn bread loaves. The next day she baked a large batch of Finnish sour cream cookies. The day after that, we loaded the chainsaw and axes in the boat and went up the Yukon River to where I had spotted a nice, dry spruce tree back in the willows. It would make good firewood. So, we tied the boat to the beach and sawed the tree into blocks that we rolled onto the boat. Mary loved every bit of it. After we got back to the village and stacked the wood in the shed, we went in for our evening meal and then to bed.

'Except a Corn of Wheat Fall'

On the next morning, a Saturday, Mary said that she didn't feel well. I took her blood pressure which seemed low, and her pulse was a bit rapid. Neither symptom seemed serious, however, so I just assumed she might be having a light case of the flu or something else. Mary rested most of the day but did get up and bake a nice chocolate cake.

That evening she didn't feel like eating supper, so she just lay on the couch and talked with us till bed time. Carol and I needed to make a phone call to our missions coordinator in Anchorage, so we went into the office to make that call.

While we were on the phone, Mary poked her head in the office and said, "I am very tired, I will make myself a piece of toast and hot milk before I go to bed." We heard her walking around and heard the toaster pop up; then there was a heavy thump sound like she had dropped something. Carol ran out of the office to see what had happened. Then she cried out, "Rick! Rick! Come out here quick. Mom has fallen on the floor!" I dropped the phone and ran into the kitchen, and there was Mary flat on her back staring at the ceiling not breathing.

Both Carol and I had taken CPR training because of our search and rescue work, so we immediately began doing CPR on her, crying out to God for help. When we realized we were getting nowhere, I ran to the CB radio, which almost everyone in the Yukon Delta had, and transmitted, "This is Pastor Rick at the Yukon Delta Assembly Mission. Carol's mother is on the floor and not breathing. Please send help immediately!"

Carol was still doing CPR when I returned. I

assisted her till the village police and health aid arrived and took over with everything they had. Then people just kept coming till the house was full of people. After about 30 minutes, the police and health aid declared Mary dead. There were no doctors nor was there a hospital in the village. We were on our own. Carol and I knelt down by Mary and prayed a prayer of thanksgiving and praise, presenting her to the Lord.

Amazingly, the whole house full of people began to pray and weep as there was such a heavy presence of the Holy Spirit. Then Sonny Joseph from the Alukanuk Assembly of God mission arrived having heard my cry on the CB radio for help. Soon the Emmonak Catholic priest also came in and asked if he could offer last rights over Mary, as nearly everyone in the house was Catholic. The Lord spoke to my heart to allow him to do so. As the priest initiated the incense ritual symbolizing prayers rising to God and praying also that the soul of the departed would rise to God, he stopped, and with tears said to me. "I don't need to do this as this woman is already with the Lord." That was very unusual for a priest to say and was a surprise to many in the house.

Everyone was numbed by what had just happened. Carol's mother lay dead on the kitchen floor. Yet the house literally erupted with praise and thanksgiving to the Lord! Then there was silence as everyone quietly wept in the presence of the Holy Spirit.

The police officer, kneeling by Mary's dead body, wept uncontrollably. He looked up at me and said through sobs, "Pastor Rick, I have attended death many times in my life, but never have I felt anything like this. What is this presence I feel so strongly?" At his statement, the people went silent, awaiting my response.

Somewhere from deep within my spirit, I began to speak words I didn't even know from where they came. I felt such an inner strength as I spoke words of Jesus' love, grace, mercy, and salvation. When I finished, Carol picked up from where I left off and ministered beautifully to those people. Then she cut the cake that Mary had baked only hours before, made some coffee, and served everyone through the night. We were up till 5:00 a.m. ministering to the people. Then the police came and took Mary's body. Finally, we went to bed for two or three hours.

On that Sunday morning, the church was filled to capacity for our service. We had a memorial service for Mary and told stories of her faith in God and her life as a farmer's wife, and as a cook at the hospital in McCall, Idaho. After the service, Carol and I crashed the rest of the day to get our strength back. What an amazing experience this had been for us and the entire village! Relationships were strengthened, and many were touched by God's amazing presence at Mary's passing. We were reminded of Jesus' words in John 12:24, "I say unto you, Except a corn of wheat fall into the ground and die, it abideth alone: but if it die, it bringeth forth much fruit."

On Monday morning, the local restaurant owner brought us a lot of food which helped out so much. Then we again packed for our trip back to Idaho for Mary's funeral. Carol and I were very fragile emotionally and cried at the drop of a hat. One concern was that we were nearly broke from all the trips we had made. Thankfully, the Alaska district purchased our airline tickets. What a blessing!

We flew straight to Boise where Carol's sister Phyllis and Vic Vaughn met us with Mary's pickup truck. She had told everyone that she wanted us to have the pickup. That was another tremendous blessing. We drove to the Maenpa home in Lake Fork and got ready for the funeral. Other family flew and drove from various parts of the country.

Gordon Coler, pastor of the McCall Assembly of God who had officiated Ted's funeral earlier that year, now led the service for Mary. All of this seemed like a sad dream from which we would wake up. But, when we awoke, it was all too real. What a different visit this was with the family as we sorted through Mary's earthly belongings and settled the estate. A new chapter had begun in all our lives.

In the days ahead, we bought an old eight-foot, over-the-cab pickup camper from my brother Art for $300. We put it on the back of Mary's pickup since we would be driving back to Alaska. The camper was in amazing shape and turned out to be a real blessing during the five-day trip back up the Alaska Highway.

After our goodbyes again to Idaho family and friends, we began our journey. The trip was much smoother than the first we'd taken 18 years before!

More Shocking News!

Upon arriving in Alaska, we went straight to the Alaska District office in Anchorage. We had no more than walked in the door when Superintendent Jack Bransford hugged us and said, "I am so sorry to give you more sad news, but your sister's husband Reginald passed away four days ago."

Grief upon grief! Again, our hearts were torn before we had a chance to heal from Mary's death. I immediately called my sister Appy Mae in Nampa, Idaho, and she told me the story of Reg's death from cardiac arrest. The funeral would be soon, but she said, "Rick, you do not need to get back on a plane and fly home for his funeral. You and Carol had a wonderful time with Reg and I just a few days ago. So, just go back to your village and preach the gospel. That is what Reg would want you to do."

So, we unloaded our camper at a dear friend's house in Anchorage and parked the pickup there also. Our son Dwight was working at McDonald's in Anchorage, so he moved into the little camper for the winter. It worked out pretty well for him.

We flew airlines back to Emmonak and took up where we had left off. It was a real blessing to see so many more people in church that had witnessed Mary's death. Her death and testimony had broken the bondage in hearts of so many of those native people. We had a powerful revival season during our last year in Emmonak.

Evangelist Warren Combs

Evangelist Warren Combs from Idaho had traveled to Alaska again for revival services during the time we were in Idaho for Mary's funeral. Upon our return, he changed some of his service dates so that I could pick him up from Point Hope village and fly him to Emmonak for a week of services before he had to return home. During his time with us, I flew him to Alakanuk, Sheldon's Point, and to Kotlik for one-night services. As was his pattern the first time he visited us in Alaska, he stood on the steps outside each mission playing his trumpet. The natives dearly loved him, his preaching, and his trumpet playing. At the conclusion of Brother Combs' visit, I flew him to Bethel for his last meeting; he then flew on home from there. What a blessing he had been to our people!

Warfare Encounter

The Kotlik mission building needed to be set level as it was built on pads that sat directly on the permafrost, which was true of most mission buildings in Alaska. So, I flew my Cherokee over to Aniak to meet with our U.S. Missions Coordinator Jim Schulz and three other MAPS workers that had been working on the Aniak mission. We flew together to Kotlik with the local missionary who had a Cessna 180. With the two planes we transported the work team to level the mission.

We had a wonderful service on one of the evenings we were there and established a few new relationships with the village people. We also had opportunity to minister to a young woman going through a great personal crisis which would become an unforgettable experience.

One evening, there was a knock at the door. When I opened the door, there stood a beautiful young Eskimo woman sobbing with a pistol aimed at her head. Through clenched teeth, she sobbed, "I don't know why I stopped here. I am on my way out of the village to end my life. There is nothing more to live for. Tell me why I stopped here; it is like some voice spoke to me to knock on your door!"

Immediately, in my spirit, I cried out to the Lord, then spoke these words, "Jesus loves you so much, He didn't want you to kill yourself. I believe that voice was Jesus speaking to your heart. Come on in and let Carol and I hear your story." Reaching toward her, I said, "Please, give me the gun." She hesitated a moment then gave the gun to me.

We went inside, and she began to pour out her soul through her tears. Drugs, alcohol, and sex had all taken their Satanic toll on her life. We read from the Scriptures of Jesus' love for even the vilest sinner. Then we prayed with her and she opened her heart to Jesus and received Him as her Savior. Soon, her face shined with God's glory and peace. She left that night singing in her heart, giving thanks to Jesus for saving her life.

But the spiritual warfare was not yet over. A few moments after the young woman went home to where her alcoholic brother also lived, the phone rang. It was her brother, and he was livid with anger. He thought I had given her some kind of powerful drug. Screaming into the phone, he said, "What did you do to my sister? She is singing, laughing, and smiling. I am going to kill you! I have a .30-30 rifle pointed at your door right now! When you come out, I am going to shoot you!"

I tried to tell him about how she had given her life to Jesus. Then I said, "Put on the coffee pot; I am coming over to visit you armed with only my Bible." I did call the village police officer as a precaution but told him not to do anything as I was going over to visit the young man.

After Carol and I prayed for God's protection, I opened the door and stepped out. No gunshot. I walked straight across to his door and knocked. When the door opened, he stood there staring at me in disbelief and said, "You're not even afraid of me, are you?"

"You can only kill the body, but not the spirit of life in me, so why should I be scared?" I replied.

"The coffee is done, come on in and let's talk," he said. So, I went in, sat down, and God calmed the young man's spirit. He listened as I told him about his sister and what had happened. He was really glad that I had taken the pistol from her and he admitted he was glad that she was so happy and not intoxicated anymore. I tried to bring him to recognize his need for Jesus, but he replied, "Not yet. I have to check this God stuff out further." I gave him a Bible and invited him to talk to me often. I wanted to be his friend.

The young man did come to our church on occasion, and one night I got him started on reading the Book of Proverbs. He was into sound thinking and rationalization, so I felt the Book of Wisdom just might jar him into seeing the Lord and his need for Him. Seed was planted, and our prayer was that the Holy Spirit would one day bring the seed to life.

A Final Tour

Our last winter and spring in Emmonak were filled with snowmobiling, flying to all the villages, and taking Jesus wherever we went. There was a sweet revival spirit among the natives, and my heart was blessed to see them digging into the deeper things of God.

We flew nine people to the Nome Eskimo Camp Meeting, and God poured out His Spirit in that week of daily services. There were several Siberian Eskimos who flew in from Saint Lawrence Island, and they were filled with the Spirit. Often the camp meetings went till the wee hours of the morning as people lingered in the presence of the Holy Spirit and hungered for more. God did a marvelous work in peoples' lives, and we were so privileged to have been part of His purposes.

Banquets and other meals at the camps were always enjoyable as well; there was always special native foods to sample. It was fun to watch different cultures try new foods prepared by Athabaskan Indian, Northern Eskimo, Yupik western Eskimo, and Siberian Eskimo groups. Sometimes, it was humorous to watch as people ate foods they had never tried before.

After returning home, Carol and I began to prepare to leave Emmonak. We surely had mixed feelings about leaving as there was such a sweet revival spirit in the village. Also, we had wanted to stick around and help get the new summer family camp going. Yet, we would soon need to leave again for Idaho to itinerate.

Days were busy with packing and moving sales. It was too costly to move large furniture, appliances, vehicles, etc., as we were 600 miles from the closest road; and everything had to come in out by air. So, it was always better to sell everything or just leave it for the next missionary.

Between packing and moving sales, we traveled to the villages as much as possible, securing the ministries at each mission as best we could. We wanted to make sure that ministry would continue after we left.

Departure day came on June 16, 1992. We had mailed all our boxes and flew our Cherokee for the last time to Aniak where Missionary Arlis Roberts took possession of "5215 Tango," the call letters for our plane. He had been a pilot during their years in Alaska and had flown a lot during those years. He also had ridden with me a number of times and loved the Cherokee. Since they had no airplane at the current time, he was very happy to get it, and we were glad to see it stay in the Lord's work. I hoped to move up to a small twin-engine airplane for overwater flights we would be making.

We already knew that the Alaska District wanted us to take Stebbins village when we returned from itineration. In fact, Carol and I made several flights to Stebbins to get a firsthand view and sense the village heartbeat. We also needed to measure the dimensions of the mission church to build a parsonage on top of the current structure.

Stebbins and nearby St. Michael are in a volcanic region with several extinct or dormant volcanoes all around. Our vision was to pastor the Stebbins mission and fly to St. Lawrence Island, some 180 miles out to sea, situated only a few miles from the Russian border. Eventually, we hoped to build an Assemblies of God mission at one or both villages on the islands of Gambell and Savoonga.

To return again to Idaho, Carol and I boarded a 737 jet and flew to Anchorage where our son Dwight had been working. We loaded all our baggage into a new Dodge Dakota 4x4 pickup we had purchased for our trip to Idaho. The trip went very well. We got almost 19 miles to the gallon and had no trouble.

Since Carol's parents were now with the Lord, we drove to Nampa and Star to visit Carol's sister Phyllis and husband, as well as my parents, Art and Appy. After a short time of rest, we picked up our 23-foot, fifth wheel trailer we had purchased earlier and began our itineration through the Southern Idaho District.

Medical Challenges

All went well until about halfway into the tour when I began to have a medical problem that puzzled the doctors. My heart beat rapidly at times and the mineral readings in my blood chemistry were out of balance. I also had high blood pressure and seemingly was developing early symptoms of dementia. I grew weak and got headaches when I was near electrical radiation from power lines, microwave ovens, televisions, cell phones, etc. I went from doctor to doctor for tests, all to no avail. I continued getting sicker and sicker.

We continued our itinerary through Idaho, then to Wyoming, and on to Michigan. By this time, I was having very serious health problem with hallucinations and fierce headaches. An Assemblies of God pastor gave me a book on chelation therapy. I read some of it but was very dubious about the treatment. The American Medical Association did not endorse chelation therapy except for lead poisoning and other heavy metal toxins.

After a number of other appointments and my health still declining, one doctor advised, "Rick, get your house in order. We have exhausted all our resources and every test is inconclusive. There is nothing more we know to do."

I took another look at the chelation therapy book and read through it slowly. Feeling I had nothing to lose, Carol and I looked up a chelation therapist about 60 miles away in Greenville, Michigan, who was one of the founding physicians in chelation treatment.

"Has anyone ever tested you for toxic metals in your blood," he asked. I replied that they had not. After taking a toxic metal blood test, I learned that I had a high level of aluminum in my blood. I had no idea as to why that would be. However, upon reviewing my medical records, the doctor noted that I had scarlet fever as a child and had rheumatic fever at age 13. I fought illness often as a child after that, and the therapist felt that my liver function had been severely hampered due to those fevers.

In addition to this, I remembered that water in Wainwright village was pumped through aluminum pipes from the fresh water ponds to the huge tanks in the village. Also, water barrels in the village were painted with aluminum oxide to keep them from rusting. Aluminum can also be absorbed into the body from some antiperspirants, aluminum fry pans, and many other sources. Considering these things, the therapist determined that it would be good to see if chelation treatments would remove the aluminum.

After the first treatment, I felt better immediately. I took two to three treatments a week for a total of 12 treatments. After the fifth treatment, my doctor took a urine sample and found a high concentration of aluminum. He was very pleased, as now he knew my body was releasing the aluminum. I couldn't believe how quickly my health improved.

Upon our return to the Southern Idaho District, I continued with chelation treatments till I completed 30 treatments. How thankful we were for God's hand of direction and healing touch!

While in Idaho, the Lord began dealing with our hearts about the church on the Fort Hall Indian reservation. Though we were still raising money for the Stebbins and St. Lawrence Island ministries in Alaska, I also knew it was unlikely that I would pass my flight medical due to my recent health issues. Since it can be very difficult to get a flight medical back after failing, I let my license lapse.

Fort Hall, Idaho

Not long after pondering and praying about ministry in Fort Hall, I got a phone call from the Southern Idaho District office asking if we would consider pastoring at Fort Hall. Unaware that the Lord had already been dealing with our hearts about Fort Hall, the superintendent said that God had spoken to him about us taking that church. He knew of my medical issues and that there would be no chelation treatments available within hundreds of miles from Stebbins village in Alaska. Carol and I wept realizing that God was again confirming His call!

During our missionary itineraries over the years, Carol and I had ministered at the Fort Hall church two or three times, so we had some idea of what would be before us. I was glad that the Lord had spoken to my heart before receiving the call from the district superintendent. This was a clear confirmation of the direction God wanted us to take. Though I knew that God certainly was able to heal me and allow us to return to Alaska, I also knew that even the Apostle Paul had pled with the Lord for healing. Yet, perhaps like Paul, God would use the "thorn in my flesh" to show that His power is made perfect in weakness. (See 2 Corinthians 12:7-10). Clearly, it seemed that the Lord saw a higher purpose for us at Fort Hall. So, after much prayer, we accepted the invitation.

Since it was too difficult and costly to move all our belongings from Alaska, we simply gave most of them to the new missionaries that came to Alaska. So, in a very real sense, we started from scratch in Fort Hall. And though this prospect was daunting, God's hand of provision became almost immediately evident. While in the Wyoming District for missionary services, the district youth director came to me and said, "God spoke to my heart that Wyoming is to pledge $5,000 toward the purchase of a Speed the Light van for you." Then the Southern Idaho District pledged the rest which enabled us to get a new 1993 Chevy Lumina van. We knew this would be a tremendous blessing in helping transport people to the mission services and for other traveling needs.

Spiritual Warfare

While delighted with our new ministry opportunity, almost immediately we began to experience spiritual warfare unlike anything we had experienced before. Spiritual oppression was so heavy at times. One evening, a police officer knocked on our door and, after introducing himself, said, "I just stopped a man dressed in a black robe coming from the house next door to your church. That man told me there were several people in that house doing animal sacrifices against you and your church. I felt you needed to know what is going on, Pastor."

Following that time, in both the church and parsonage, we experienced a heavy infestation of black widow spiders as well as the very poisonous hobo spider. Additionally, the grass around the church was dead, as were all the flowers. Briars, thistles, and puncture weeds were everywhere.

Soon I learned that there was also a Satan worship house on the south side of us. Medicine men were doing strange rituals against the church. In the midst of all this, Carol was stricken with a very strange affliction. She was unable to eat, could not sleep, and became very depressed. She began to lose weight and vomit frequently. The doctors were stumped, unable to determine what was wrong. As Carol's condition worsened, they admitted her to a mental hospital in Pocatello for evaluation and treatment. This was a very dark time for me, but it drove me and our church to pray like never before.

As the spiritual warfare intensified during Carol's hospitalization, I was awakened by owls hooting from the trees behind the parsonage. The native people were terrified of owls hooting in the night over a house. According to their beliefs, it meant death was coming to that house. Then one night, about 4:00 a.m., I heard a strange fluttering sound of wings by the church. I stepped out of the house and saw a number of hawks swooping over the church. They would fly in an east to west direction, then switch to a north to south direction. Feeling a heavy, evil presence, I began to rebuke the owls and the hawks in Jesus' name. Immediately, the birds fled to the north.

The next morning, a young native junior high-age boy who always liked to stop by the parsonage for a cup of hot chocolate, ran past the parsonage without even looking at me. I ran after him and asked, "What is wrong? Why did you run by and not stop for hot chocolate this morning?" The young boy looked at me terrified, and said, "They put the hawks on you last night. I was afraid to stop since they put a curse on you."

"It doesn't matter," I told him. "The hawks and owls went away when I cried out, 'In Jesus' name, I rebuke you!' They are gone, and I am alive, because greater is he that is in me than he that is in the world."

When I learned that the insurance would no longer pay for Carol's stay at the hospital, I brought her home. She was heavily sedated on strong medicines; yet, when we went to bed, I was awakened by her crying and praying. She cried, "Lord, if You are not going to heal me, then please just take me home to heaven. I cannot suffer any more!" She went into the living room and collapsed on the living room floor crying. All I could do was just give her to Jesus.

This became an all-out battle for Carol's life, way past any medical help, bigger than any doctor or hospital. I ran to the phone and called the church people and many others. People all over the nation were on their faces praying for Carol during that time. Soon the parsonage was filled with people on their faces crying out to Jesus to heal Carol and set her free!

On my face before God I prayed, "Lord, if you desire to take Carol home, I give her to You. I will do this work You have called me to do alone if I must." Then the Lord spoke to me. "*My son, you have said what I wanted to hear you say. Now that you have given her to Me, I am giving her back to you!*"

Healing and deliverance came almost at once to Carol. Just then, Carol's niece, Connie Vaughn from Nampa called and said, "God just gave me a vision of where Carol is lying on the floor. A fountain of God's glory is springing up from where she lays, flowing down the streets in every direction bringing healing wherever that fountain goes." From that day, God poured strength into Carol. She became a pillar of godly strength and encouragement to every soul she touches.

Jericho March

Though we had experienced a powerful breakthrough, spiritual warfare continued to rage on. One Sunday night, I felt compelled of the Spirit to buy a gallon of cooking oil and place it on the altar. I called the church body to pray over the oil, stating that, as a church body, we had been attacked by Satan like never before. After prayer, we went outside. I punched a small hole in the plastic jug and we began a silent Jericho march around the church property allowing the oil to flow out onto the ground. Seven times we silently marched around the church property with the oil draining. After the seventh lap, we went into the church and began to shout, sing, and praise the Lord! As we did, the glory of the Lord came down!

We prayed for the witch doctors that were doing evil against us that God would make them see the folly of their ways and repent; and if they did not, that God would remove them. Within one week, the man on the north side died suddenly. The man on the south side left town. No one knew where he went. There was a fresh sense of the Holy Spirit's move in our church. We began a concert of prayer on Thursday nights and people from all over the valley came. Services often went till midnight. We saw miraculous healings during that time.

Amazing Transformation

One beautiful spring morning, I walked our Schnauzer, Kavik, around the church yard. I noticed that all the flowers were beautiful, the grass was green, the trees were all in beautiful bloom, and there were no spiders! Then, as I walked around the north side of the property, I noticed that in the yard where the witch doctor had been, the grass was dead, there were no flowers, and the yard was full of briars. Of the eight trees around his house that were lush and beautiful the summer before, seven of them were dead from the roots up! One tree was in beautiful bloom. Wondering about the significance of this, I recalled that seven is God's perfect number, and that eight signifies a new beginning. I began to shout and praise the Lord. Certainly, if God was for us, then who could stand against us! Soon afterward, a Caterpillar operator knocked down the witch doctor's house and filled in the hole. He also took down the seven dead trees and cleaned up the yard.

Connecting with the Culture

Early in our ministry in Fort Hall, God spoke to Carol and me about something that seemed very foreign to us—to minister Jesus Christ to Native Americans in the context of their culture. I struggled with this and questioned God about how this could be, believing that the spiritual practices of the Native American culture were sinful and could not be incorporated into presenting the gospel. Yet, God impressed upon my heart that the culture itself was not sinful, but that Native American worship focused on Creation instead of the Creator and His only begotten Son Jesus Christ.

In Deuteronomy 4:15-19, God instructed Moses, *"Take ye therefore good heed unto yourselves, for ye saw no manner of similitude on the day that the LORD spoke unto you in Horeb out of the midst of the fire: Lest ye corrupt yourselves, and make you a graven image, the similitude of any figure, the likeness of male or female. The likeness of any beast that is on the earth, the likeness of any winged fowl that flieth in the air, the likeness of any thing that creepeth on the ground, the likeness of any fish that is in the waters beneath the earth: And lest thou lift up thine eyes unto heaven, and when thou seest the sun, and the moon, and the stars, even at the host of heaven, shouldest be driven to worship them, and serve them, which the LORD thy God hath divided unto all nations under the whole heaven."*

Though the native people were sincere in their worship, it was misdirected. They needed to understand that the earthly creation and the heavenly realms are not to be worshiped themselves, but they are to ascribe worship to God. Psalm 148:1-13 declares that all of the created order is to worship Him—the sun, moon, and stars; the oceans, mountains, and hills; all creatures on land and in the seas; all of humankind, and more. All are to give praise to the Lord!

Then this directive came, "*Let them worship Me in native song and with dance.*"

Despite these words from God, I still struggled with their native forms of dance and worship. "Lord!" I cried, "they dance with large drums and unusual beats, and wear strange clothing and feathers!" Then He reminded me of Psalm 149:3, 4, where He calls on His people to dance and to make music; to play music with "the timbrel and harp," for He delights in this. Psalm 150:3-6, further instructs praising God with the trumpet, pipe, and cymbals as well as stringed instruments and with dancing.

So, I had to ask myself, *"Are the Native Americans the only people on the face of the earth that cannot dance their native dance or sing their native songs in praise to the King of kings and Lord of lords?"*

During that time, a number of gospel singing groups and bands were putting religious words to contemporary music in an effort to bring the youth to Jesus. I was still from the old school, as was most of our support base. Similarly, it seemed that as we used native dance and music to reveal Jesus Christ, God was using it to bring Native Americans to the Lord. However, when some of our supporting churches heard about what we were doing, they dropped our support. During the first few months of pioneering this new ministry, we lost over $1,000 in monthly support. Even the district office indicated that they were going to wait and see what kind of fruit would be borne of this new thing.

As Carol and I sought the Lord for direction, I learned about an evangelist and nationally appointed home missionary, Art Begay, who also was a full-blooded Native American. We invited him to come and conduct a week-long revival with us at Fort Hall. I soon realized that he had the same calling and vision that Carol and I had. Art had such a deep knowledge of Native American history and cultural values that I realized this had to be God bringing us together. We wept and prayed together for the salvation of lost native tribes. As we worked together, Art choreographed dance and drama performances that our youth could present at churches, parks, and Pow Wows around the nation.

'Warriors for Christ'

Two weeks before the large Fort Hall Native American Pow Wow, where some 30 different Indian tribes would be dressed in their cultural regalia and present native dance and music, Art and I felt we needed to have a "Warriors for Christ" drama and dance team ready for this event. But, we also knew that the planning committee had never allowed any church or Christian group to participate in the Pow Wow. So, we prayed and cried out to the Lord for direction and favor with the committee. Also, Art did not have a final choreograph for the group worked out until he began his drive from Columbia Falls, Montana, to Fort Hall. As God spoke to him along the way, he would stop and write. This went on until he arrived at Fort Hall a week before the Pow Wow.

We assembled a performance team among our youth, which we named "Warriors for Christ," and practiced the new drama and dance. Our opening drama/dance was called "The Good Dance." Our group would dance into the center of the arena, and through native drama/dance, portray the atrocities of war, death, alcohol, drugs, and ungodly immoral relationships. The next act presented the "answer" portraying Jesus being beaten and nailed to the Cross. This was followed by His death, resurrection, and the worship of the risen Savior Jesus Christ by all native people everywhere. I portrayed the role of the missionaries who brought the Holy Bible and the message of Jesus Christ to the native people.

Art and I made several calls and visits to an area Pow Wow director for permission to perform. Finally, the day came, and we were ready. However, as we started for the Pow Wow grounds, we felt nervous, even fearful. We sensed that Satan was not happy with what was about to happen. Then, unexpectedly, the Pow Wow director came and said, "You cannot dance at our Pow Wow." No explanation was given.

Greatly perplexed by what had just happened, we loaded up the van and went back to the church. The entire Warriors team began to pray. After about an hour the phone rang; it was the Pow Wow director. "I don't know what is going on," she said, "but our lead dance team's bus just broke down about an hour out of Fort Hall. They can't make it for the opening events. So, we decided to let your Warriors for Christ perform instead. Get here as fast as you can!"

We all jumped back into the Speed the Light van and sped off to the Pow Wow grounds, all the while praising God and worshiping the Lord! When we got out and quickly gathered at the entrance area, it seemed as if Satan began filling our team with a great fear. One by one the Warriors began to shy away and try to hide. Clearly, the enemy was totally upset that we would be presenting Jesus in a Native American way to people he sought to control.

Christian Indian prayer warriors began to gather around our group and pray out loud. Soon, the Warriors team calmed down and, with tears in their eyes, prepared to dance as our music began to play in the arena. The moment we began our dance, all fear was gone!

A strange hush came over the crowd as we performed our drama and dance. After our performance, there was a thundering applause and loud cries of approval from the crowd. Native people grabbed the Warriors and hugged them, many weeping. When the announcer came on, he stammered, not knowing what to say. Then the Pow Wow queen asked the Warriors for Christ to perform again the next evening. So, the next evening they performed again before an estimated 6,000 people from some 30 tribes around the nation!

After our presentation, we were invited to perform at the Browning, Montana, Blackfeet Nation Pow Wow. We also received several invitations to other native events. But, I was not prepared for the opportunity that was about to unfold.

A 'Super' Invitation

About a month after the Fort Hall Pow Wow, I answered the phone in my office and a lady on the other end of the line said, "I am the events coordinator for Super Bowl XXX with the Pittsburgh Steelers and Dallas Cowboys at Tempe, Arizona. How are you?" Thinking this was a prank, I answered, "I'm the President of the United States of America. How are you?"

"No, I am who I say," she said. "Super Bowl XXX will be honoring Native American heritage and cultural values in the pregame ceremonies. I have heard from numerous tribal Indian chiefs from around the nation about your dance team. We would be honored if you would bring them to the Super Bowl Pow Wow the day before the Super Bowl game and do a full performance at that event. We also would like your team to dance during the pregame activities before the ball game on Sunday."

What an unbelievable opportunity for ministry! My head was spinning! "Sure!" I said. But, my mind was screaming, "How?"

Miraculous Provision

Soon after, I received a call from the Speed the Light office. "Brother Rick, we just received $24,000 for your Speed the Light account, but we don't know how it got there. Do you need a bigger van?"

"Yes!" I said. So, I was instructed to drive our Lumina van to Los Angeles and give it to a U.S. missionary there, then fly from Los Angeles to Springfield to pick up a new Ford, 15-passenger van for the Warriors for Christ team.

So, Carol and I did just that. Speed the Light bought our tickets to fly from Los Angeles to Springfield. We stayed there and visited Carol's brother and wife, John and Jan Maempa for a few days before heading home with our new 1995 Ford 350 van.

Invitations Abound

Things really began to move quickly with Warriors for Christ. I received calls from churches all over the district to have services with them to hear our story and witness the Warriors perform.

After returning with our new van, we began to pray for finances to cover the cost of all the invitations for ministry we were receiving. We were so blessed as the churches gave us good offerings; even the Native American events covered our expenses as well.

Soon, we would be fulfilling the invitation to the Blackfeet Nation Pow Wow in Browning, Montana. The invitation had come from Earl Old Person, chairman of the Blackfeet Tribal Council and honorary lifetime Chief of the Blackfeet Nation.

When we arrived in Browning, it was quite cold, so the pow wow was held in a large building at the fairgrounds. We had practiced much and upgraded the drama/dance routine.

Heavy Anointing

When it was our turn to perform, as in Fort Hall, the entire arena became quiet as our music began. There was a heavy anointing of the Holy Spirit on the song. I tried hard to hold back the tears as we ministered.

After we danced off the arena, Chief Earl Old Person grabbed the microphone and said, "Warriors for Christ, come back up here now!" My heart jumped into my throat as I didn't know why he had called us back. There was silence in the crowd. The most powerful man in the Blackfeet Nation had spoken.

After we lined up along the front, Chief Earl Old Person came to us in his beautiful full head dress and regalia and hugged each of our youth with a long and warm embrace. He didn't say a word until he stood in front of me. Then he hugged me and said in a loud and clear voice, "Never have I seen God like I saw Him today. Thank you for being obedient to the Lord and putting together such a performance that has moved the Natives across this land. God richly bless you!" At that, the crowd went wild; a procession began with all the people coming in front of us and throwing money onto an Indian blanket. Chief Earl Old Person picked up the blanket, tied it around the cash, and handed it to us and said, "Use this money to pay for your trip to the Super Bowl Pow Wow in Tempe, Arizona!" This was an unbelievable expression of love from this great Native American nation and its leader!

Invitation from TBN

After returning home from Montana, the phone rang again. This time it was a representative from the Trinity Broadcasting Network satellite station in Seattle, Washington.

"After you return from your Super Bowl performance in Tempe, Arizona," the caller said, "we want you to bring the Warriors for Christ and perform on TBN television here in Seattle." Again, I was speechless and marveled at the doors God was opening!

Though the open doors were amazing, our time at home was being stretched to the limit. In the midst of all the performances and outreach ministries that the Warriors for Christ were doing, we still had a church to pastor in Fort Hall. So, sometimes we sent the team out on ministry without us.

On to Super Bowl XXX

With the Super Bowl in Tempe almost upon us, we had a lot to get ready, including making new regalia for the Warriors. So, the church ladies and Women's Ministries members worked sometimes into the wee hours of the morning to get the outfits ready. They did beautiful work. Soon it was time to go.

First Assembly of God church in Pocatello, Idaho, wanted us to present our Super Bowl choreography and ministry before we left for Tempe. God moved powerfully in that service! People wept and prayed and ran to the altar. That spoke volumes to the team. Then the church gave us a wonderful offering to add to what we had received in Browning.

As we left for Tempe, the weather deteriorated. We left in a snow storm and drove for 21 hours straight through to Tempe. Totally exhausted, we were glad to turn in for the night and get a nice long sleep.

When we arrived at the pow wow grounds, we were amazed again as Art was asked to be the lead dancer, heading the entire pow wow! This shocked Art and me to the point that we had to pray through on this. Art agreed to take the lead. Going to the microphone, he addressed the Pow Wow saying, "I want to thank my Lord and Savior Jesus Christ for the opportunity to lead the first dance at this great event." Then he prayed in Jesus' name. I don't believe that has ever been done at any pow wow anywhere nor at a Super Bowl event. We had 21 dancers on the Warriors for Christ team in beautiful regalia for this event. What a powerful time of ministry this was unto Jesus Christ our Lord!

On Saturday, all of the native dancers were to practice for the Super Bowl pregame performance. The Warriors had to be in their regalia all day and were transported to the Sun Devil Stadium in school busses. Hundreds of Indian dancers performed. The actual performances lasted only a few minutes, but to get them all organized and working together took hours! During the activities, some of the Warriors got to meet briefly with the Dallas Cowboys and Pittsburg Steelers, which was a pretty big deal for them. But the miracle of it all was the fact that Jesus was lifted up at the most influential Pow Wow ever. That was awesome!

Trinity Broadcasting Network

As soon as we returned home, we began to prepare for an opportunity to appear on the Trinity Broadcasting Network. This trip to TBN's Seattle, Washington studio would be another one in the dead of winter and would require at least three vehicles to carry the performers and luggage.

Two large churches wanted us for services while we were in Seattle, so we left several days early. One church allowed us to camp out in their dining hall. It was so awesome to watch the response of the congregations that had never seen a Native American team perform a native dance and drama unto Jesus Christ the Lord. They would come to the altar after the service and cry out to Jesus. We always gave an altar call after the services and offered prayer for peoples' healing.

After arriving for the studio taping, there was little time to rest. We arose around 5:00 a.m. so we could get showered, have breakfast, and get to the studio by 7:00 a.m. All the Warriors had to get their long hair braided and don their native regalia for the performance.

TBN planned to tape the performance so that they could correct any mistakes or make changes. There were many stops and redo's as the producers wanted everything perfect. The Warriors became exhausted after dancing for hours. But, eventually, it was finished, and the end result was awesome!

The next morning, TBN invited Art and me to come for a half-hour live interview about the Warriors for Christ ministry. The Warriors were there, but in street clothes in the audience. During our interview, I noticed that most of the people taking prayer calls were busy on the phones. Afterward, the producers hugged our necks and said, "This was one of the most awesome programs we have ever done!" We found out later that they played the tape four times because of demand.

On the way home, we stopped at a men's retreat in McCall, Idaho, and performed our ministry for some 500 men there. Art Begay spoke at the gathering. What a move of God we had in those meetings!

Memorable Moments

Many services with the Warriors followed at other pow wows, fairs, schools, holiday performances, too many to relate in detail. Some events, however, were particularly memorable.

After ministering at a Pow Wow in South Dakota, many native people wanted to talk about the Lord and ask about our ministry. Some wondered how they could start a similar ministry. During the meeting, we met the "Risen Warriors," a singing ministry team. On Sunday morning, we had a service on the reservation under a tree. Many people from the Pow Wow attended. It was a great service!

On the way home, we traveled through Wounded Knee Reservation. As soon as we crossed onto the reservation, a sad, heavy spirit weighed down all of us. As I looked over the grounds, I could see what appeared to be something wavy rising off the ground. As I began to pray, I sensed God speaking to my heart saying, *"These are the cries of the innocent blood that was spilled here rising from the ground. This is what I felt when Abel's blood in Genesis cried out to me from the ground."* I told the Warriors about what I had sensed, and they, as with one voice, began to weep and pray for the salvation of the living on that reservation. We wept and prayed all the way across the reservation.

U.S. Missions Presentation

After the U. S. Missions Department learned of our many Warriors for Christ events, I was asked to speak about this new ministry to other U.S. missionaries at a Missions Institute in Springfield, Missouri. Two other missionaries that were doing new things were also asked to speak.

During the meeting, we were placed at a table before the entire delegation for a question and answer panel. Most of the attendees agreed with what we were doing; a small percentage, however, struggled with the concept of using native dance and culture to minister to Native Americans.

We certainly understood their concerns. Most of the delegates who took issue were dear native brothers that had come from the old school, as we had. They had forsaken any form of their native cultural dance, fearing that to accommodate it in any form would draw them back into the evil spiritual influences from which they had been delivered. Some would no longer wear Native American dress of any kind. Carol and I respected their concerns. They were our brothers, and we loved them. They would be able to touch the hearts and souls of native people that we could never reach. Yet, I have thought often of a story told me by a native in Fort Hall several years before we went there to minister. His story is as follows:

"I was a hopeless drunk and miserable in my sin and in need of a Savior," he said. *"I came to this church one Sunday morning and was moved by the Holy Spirit. I came forward and gave my life to Jesus. Sometime later, I came back and asked the missionary if I could give my testimony and play the song, "The Old Rugged Cross," on my Indian flute. He told me that my long hair was shameful and that I would have to burn my Indian flute as there were evil spirits in it. I walked out of the church and never went back."* Then he added, *"But guess what. I never turned my back on Jesus! I just gave my instruments to the Lord and used them for His glory."*

Pentecostal Evangel Interview

During much of our time in Fort Hall, my brother-in-law John Maempa was managing editor of the *Pentecostal Evangel*. In September 1996, he transitioned from there to serve as editor of *Mountain Movers*, then the official magazine for the Division of Foreign Missions. On a visit to Springfield, John arranged for me to be interviewed for a news article in the *Pentecostal Evangel* titled, "*Rick Rigenhagen discusses ministry to Native Americans*." It appeared in the January 19, 1997 issue.

In the article, I said, "*We are careful to separate*

Indian culture from religion, because idolatrous Indian religion cannot be redeemed for Jesus Christ. The Lord spoke to my heart to take the Indian culture and redeem it for Him. It is no different than taking a piano, guitar, drum set out of a night club and taking to the altar of Jesus Christ where it can now be used for God's glory.

For the most part, the Native American community has been thankful and respectful of our presentation. But, some Native American Christians have yet to become excited because of a concern that we are trying to mix two religions; Christianity and Indian religion. This is called syncretism. If we had done this, we would have disgraced what Jesus did on the Cross."

Winds of Change

Carol and I were so grateful to be part of something God was using in a powerful way to reach the precious Native American culture for Christ. Yet, almost unperceptively at first, winds of change in our ministry began to blow as God began to prepare us for further direction in ministry.

Carol and I began to notice that there were a lot of motorcycle riders in the southeastern Idaho area, and riding motorcycles is something I have always enjoyed.

One day, I noticed an ad in the paper for a 1982 Honda 650 Nighthawk. It appeared to be in great shape and was reasonably priced; so, we went to look at it. I took it for a test ride and fell in love with it. It was so good to have a motorcycle again after all these years.

It was early summer, and I enjoyed getting up early in the morning and riding through the twisting, paved mountain roads in the Pocatello area. I especially loved riding up to the Mink Creek area and praying on the mountaintop overlooking the Pocatello/Fort Hall area.

Soon I learned that there were several secular motorcycle clubs and groups in the region, but there was no Christian group. A burden for the unsaved motorcycle riders began to settle into my spirit; they seemed so lost. As I prayed, I wept before the Lord and began to wonder why I was so burdened for them.

Soon after these initial times of prayer, I noticed a little ad in the local newspaper stating that the Tri-state coordinator and the president of the Twin Falls chapter of the Christian Motorcycle Association (CMA) were organizing an informational and promotional meeting in the area about CMA. So, Carol and I went to the meeting. As I listened, I knew in my heart that God was about to move our ministry in a different direction. Carol and I joined CMA and received patches to place on our vests.

Wanting to get started, we inquired about forming a CMA ride group in Pocatello. We were quickly approved to do so. Soon afterward, we put an ad in the paper that stated if any motorcycle riders were interested in riding with a Christian group to meet at the Wal-Mart parking lot at 6:30 every Friday night. We would have a tour followed by dinner and Christian fellowship. Five bikers showed up the first night. We rode up on a mountain above the city and, as the sun set and city lights came on below, we had a great time of prayer over the valley. Then we had dinner together before going home.

We grew quickly with eight to ten riders attending regularly. Then, the local leader of "March for Jesus" asked us if we would like to ride our motorcycles and lead the group through the city of Pocatello. We would end the ride by stopping at the park for a chili feed and fellowship. We were very glad to participate.

ABATE Jack

About halfway through the "March for Jesus" ride, we were abruptly halted by a biker called "ABATE Jack" from a notorious secular group.

ABATE is an acronym that originally stood for "American Bikers Against Totalitarian Enactments." Members of this group generally opposed regulations such as helmet laws, motorcycle safety inspections, rider training and licensing, and more.

Riding right up to us, Jack stopped the march and

asked what we were doing. I quickly explained the ride and invited him to ride at the front with us and join us for the chili feed at the park. Our invitation and honoring him in that manner softened opposition to CMA activities. Jack rode with us to the park, stayed to eat, and talked with us. Before we left, he hugged our necks and invited us to ride in the "Toys for Tots" run for Christmas toys for needy children in the area. He also invited our group to their chili feed and party after the toy run. This was our first invitation to any secular event by the local biker clubs.

When the time came for the Toys for Tots run, we rode with Jack and his group and thoroughly enjoyed the experience. At the party afterward, I noticed that every club stayed in their little groups, not mingling with others. In fact, there seemed to be friction in the air.

Abate Jack and some of his group started a fire outside to roast wieners and marshmallows. Picnic tables also were set up for places to eat. Then Jack suddenly stood up on a block of wood and shouted loudly at the group with a spiel of profanities, telling everyone to gather in because Chaplain Rick was going to pray over our event and food. This was a first! I had never been introduced like that before. I had no idea that Jack wanted me to pray!

Everyone gathered close by and things got stone quiet. In my heart I was praying a hundred miles per hour; I had no idea what to say or expect. I thanked

Jack for the invitation and gave about a thirty-second personal introduction and told them about our CMA group. I also invited them to ride with us anytime and let them know that they could come to us for prayer for their needs. Then I prayed over the event and the food. This proved to be another huge means of breaking down barriers. Many bikers gathered around and just wanted me to share my heart with them. God works in such awesome ways!

As the weather became wintry, we didn't ride as much, but we had indoor fellowships and planning meetings. Then a man named Harry Lord and his wife Sheri from Idaho Falls came over to talk about joining up with us. They had previously been outlaw motorcycle club members and had a rough background. However, they had found Christ as Savior and had joined with CMA. They also had started a ride group in Idaho Falls about two years after Carol and I started one in Pocatello. As both groups began to grow, the CMA tri-state coordinator suggested that the Idaho Falls group join with us. So, we began having monthly meeting in Blackfoot which is midway between Pocatello and Idaho Falls.

Harry and Sheri's involvement was a really good move for all of us at that time, As the ride group grew, I asked for charter member chapter status from CMA headquarters which was granted. Harry was elected president of the group and I served as chaplain. Soon, the ride group began to grow in number and spirit. At the Tri-State CMA Rally in

Twin Falls, we were chartered as "The Damascus Road Riders" chapter.

Gathering of Many Nations

Although Carol and I were getting more and more involved with biker ministry, we continued to pastor Fort Hall Assembly and went on most of the Warriors for Christ trips. However, the Warriors were able to travel to many of the events on their own. As that ministry expanded, we certainly had to pray continually for the team as Satan was not happy that so many Native Americans were coming to Christ.

At one point, the Warriors received an invitation to travel to Hemet, California, for the "Gathering of Many Nations." Tribes and bands of Native Americans would be there from all over the nation. Meetings were to be held in a large tent that would seat many hundreds.

When our group performed their ministry, the entire Native gathering erupted in praise and began dancing in the Spirit. Then the Holy Spirit fell on us all and people fell to the ground, lost in the presence of God. Most of the Warriors were slain in the Spirit for hours. Many were so drunk in the Spirit they couldn't walk for hours.

On the following night, both ends of the tent suddenly were rolled up and hundreds of Native American people from two different tribes entered.

These tribes were still embroiled in conflicts that had begun hundreds of years before. Facing each other, each tribe carried spears and ancient weapons of war. Then the chiefs of each tribe, beautifully dressed in their buckskins with eagle feather head dresses, led the way as, one by one, the tribe members piled their weapons on the ground in front of each other. Weeping profusely and with passionate hugs, they gave each other gifts and cried out, "We will fight no more! The war of ages will end here tonight. We will become one in Christ Jesus from this day forward! The war is over!" The presence of the Holy Spirit during those meetings was unlike anything I had ever seen or experienced.

While in California, a local pastor asked me to bring the Warriors to his church on a Sunday morning. After the performance and message, the people came and hugged the Warriors and wept before the Lord.

Growing Acceptance

After arriving back home, the Warriors were invited to perform their ministry at Southern Idaho District Council in Twin Falls. Some area pastors and laypeople still had reservations about this "new thing" God was doing, incorporating Native culture in our ministry. However, after that council, we no longer heard negative comments from people in our district.

Later, we were invited to perform at the Wyoming

District Council. The next morning, we were invited to the First Assembly of God church kitchen where the district superintendent personally prepared our breakfast! We had so many awesome experiences those days. We prayed for a lot of people and saw many healings and salvations. How thankful and blessed we were! Carol and I were so grateful to be part of something God was using in such a powerful way to reach the precious Native American culture for Christ. Yet, almost unperceptively at first, winds of change in our ministry again began to blow as God further directed our steps.

Shortly afterward, Art Begay was invited to take a small group of the Warriors for Christ to Hawaii for ministry performances. God really moved on the Hawaiian natives during that time. This ministry was an expression of thanks to the Hawaiian "Island Breeze" Christian dance team that had performed the gospel message in native Hawaiian cultural dance and drama in American Falls and at the Fort Hall reservation previously. Seeing their performance really sealed in my heart that this was what God wanted us to do with the Native Americans.

"Stand in the Gap" Gathering

Our Warriors ministry was rising about the same time as the greatly popular Promise Keepers men's gatherings that were taking place across the nation. On one occasion, Art was asked to have a major part in the "Sacred Assembly of Men" on the Mall in Washington, D.C., on October 4, 1997. Called "Stand in the Gap," this gathering urged men to repent and turn to Jesus Christ as Lord of their lives. Five of us flew to Washington for that great gathering.

Native Americans were given strong visibility and participation in the event. At least eighteen large, white Indian prayer tee-pees were scattered all through the Mall, leading up to our nation's capitol building. A prayer over the event was offered by an Indian chief dressed in native regalia. Art Begay also was dressed in his regalia and played "Amazing Grace" on his Indian flute. The Holy Spirit came so heavily upon that event that, as one man, the entire gathering of more than one million strong, went to their knees, weeping and crying out to the Lord in repentance, healing, and reconciliation.

At one point, a large group of gay activists and atheists gathered in front of the platform and became very disrespectful and disruptive. In response, thousands of praying men locked arms and encircled the group and began to rebuke the spirit of Satan. Eventually, the activists settled down and remained quiet during the rest of the event.

Attacks of the Enemy

During the six years Carol and I ministered at Fort Hall and the five years we were with Warriors for

Christ, we experienced many strange spiritual encounters. Some of these encounters certainly reflected the words of 1 Peter 5:8, *"Be sober, be vigilant; because your adversary the devil, as a roaring lion, walketh about, seeking whom he may devour."*

Clearly, the enemy did not like what we were doing. I personally experienced evil spirit visitations. Sometimes the enemy tried to violently stop what we were doing. But, through the power of the Holy Spirit in Jesus' name, we got the victory!

On one occasion we took the Warriors team to Hungry Horse, Montana, for the Convocation of Native Americans at the large Christian campground there. For me, these trips were very busy and sometimes frustrating trying to keep everything organized. We had to keep the Warriors fed and have places to sleep; the performances had to be organized. All of this could be very physically and emotionally demanding.

On that ministry trip, before the evening service, I had an hour or so to lie down for a few minutes on my bunk. But, as soon as I laid down, suddenly something began to physically hit me with what felt like a baseball bat. Every place I was hit hurt terribly, and a welt would rise up and turn black and blue. Though it was broad daylight, I could not see who or what was hitting me.

As I sensed the awful presence of an evil spirit, I

began to cry out rebuking the spirit in Jesus' name. People outside heard me and came running in. I told them to pray and read and quote the Word of God. I didn't even believe Satan had that kind of authority over me as a born again child of God. Soon, the beatings ceased, but I hurt all over. Then the Holy Spirit came upon me, and I, along with the people in my room, began to rejoice and praise the Lord! Most of the welts went away almost immediately.

Special Visitation

That night as the Warriors performed and ministered at the Convocation, a powerful spirit of praise and worship came over the congregation. During the presentation, the Warriors washed the feet of our native evangelist; there wasn't a dry eye in the place.

At breakfast the next morning, one of the Warriors rushed into the dining room and said, "Quick, Pastor Rick, I think there is an angel outside talking to the Warriors!"

I dropped everything and quickly went outside to see for myself. I saw a fair-complected man with shoulder-length blond hair and blue eyes. He had a kind, sweet spirit as he ministered to the Warriors that were around him. When he saw me, he smiled and began to speak a blessing and words of wisdom to me. I felt very blessed during that awesome moment as I closed my eyes in prayer. When I opened my eyes, the man was gone.

That evening, in a town a few miles away, we had another service. As the Warriors began their ministry routine, I spotted the same blond-haired, blue-eyed man standing in the doorway behind the congregation. Looking our way, he nodded his head gently and smiled. He then turned and went outside and I never saw him again.

Warriors to Alaska

As our time in Fort Hall and with Warriors for Christ began to draw to an end, we had the awesome opportunity to take the team to Alaska where Carol and I began our ministry and spent 20 amazing years with the native cultures there. The trip to Fairbanks was a beautiful experience for the Warriors. Most of the mountains in Alaska are so huge, such as Mount McKinley that soars some 20,000 feet. The team saw beautiful, deep gorges crossed by high bridges, lakes and glaciers. They saw many moose and mountain sheep.

While in Fairbanks, we were able to attend the evening services of Richard Twiss' Wiconi International Ministries, though we did not perform the first night. Wiconi means "life" in the Lakota/Sioux language.

The next day was filled with many different tribes worshiping Christ Jesus in their tribal, cultural ways. When the Warriors performed their dance/drama, the crowd again erupted in praise and worship unto the Lord. A number of Assembly of God pastors and church members were there observing the cultural worship expressions for the first time.

On the final day there, we were invited by KJNP (King Jesus North Pole), a 50,000-watt AM/FM Christian radio and television station that broadcasts from North Pole. On live television I was interviewed by Dick Olson, station manager, whom I had known for many years. Warriors also gave their testimonies of what Jesus had done in their lives. Then, on Sunday morning, we performed our ministry at the Native Assembly of God in Fairbanks, and I preached the Word. Oh, the Lord came down in that meeting! After the service, many native people came forward for prayer, healing, and deliverance.

After the convention, I drove the Warriors around Fairbanks and out to Fox to see the Alaska pipeline up close. They were blown away by it all. Then, we went downtown Fairbanks to Graehl Assembly of God where our Alaska ministry began with helping Dale Umphrey build that church. I wanted to see if the 300-pound rock I dragged and rolled out of a gravel pit for the foundation was still there. It was still there! What a memory!

From there, we all went to Fairbanks International Airport and flew back to Seattle, Washington.

Motorcycle and Prison Chaplaincy

Upon returning from the trip to Alaska with the Warriors, God really began to speak to Carol and I again about motorcycle ministry. We knew that, once more, we would be fire starters, igniting something new. We would be launching out into Motorcycle Chaplaincy under Assemblies of God U.S. Missions. With this new calling in view, we would need to hand the torch of ministry in Fort Hall to the Warriors for Christ team and allow them to continue the ministry they had been doing so well. So, in late November 1999, Carol and I resigned as pastor of Fort Hall Assembly of God and moved into our 23-foot fifth wheel trailer to begin our new ministry.

Sadly, when news of our transition to motorcycle ministry became known, we began receiving phone calls and letters from some supporters that felt like we were entering a "non-ministry" and, therefore, they would not continue their financial support. This was similar to the response we received early in our launch of Warriors for Christ.

Again, our support dropped at least $1,000 a month for many months. Though very difficult, we could understand this, as truly this was another "new thing" God was doing in the Assemblies of God.

We were invited to park our fifth-wheel trailer at a Church of God in Pocatello. From there, wearing our new CMA patches, we expanded our ministry to bikers. We also began taking Jesus into jails in Bannock County, American Falls, Blackfoot, and Idaho Falls. We immediately realized that when we put on our biker apparel, we were accepted into the bikers' world.

After staying two weeks at the Church of God, some friends from Pocatello invited us to park our trailer in their yard and plug into their house electricity for the winter. What a blessing that was! From there, we began to get invitations to speak around the district and at city functions.

As the snow began to fall and the roads slickened, there was little motorcycle riding; however, we had regular CMA gatherings in Blackfoot and in Idaho Falls at the CMA president's home. The Damascus Road Riders chapter was growing in membership and in the power of the Lord monthly.

During the Southern Idaho District Council in the spring, I was approached by Eldon Isaak who had his home and owned apartments in Rockland. He invited Carol and me to store our fifth wheel there and live in a one-bedroom apartment free of charge.

All we had to do was cover utilities and mow the grass around the property. That was awesome! The only downside to this was that we were now some 50 miles from Pocatello where most of our ministry was taking place. But, it didn't take us long to realize that God was even using us at Rockland to touch lives for Jesus Christ. A small church in the area was without a pastor for a time, so Carol and I filled in until they were able to secure a pastor, which was an added blessing.

As the ministry progressed, I found myself very busy visiting the motorcycle gang members as well as inmates in jail. God moved in those times in such powerful ways. Many times I had to pull off the road on the way home from services and classes in jail, weeping and praising God over the souls saved and delivered!

Matter of Life and Death

One afternoon, I was outside mowing the grass when, suddenly, God spoke to my heart, "*Get to Bannock County jail now*!" That voice came so strongly that I shut off the mower and ran into the house and told Carol what God just said to me. She immediately pointed to the motorcycle and said, "Go! Go! Go!!" She felt the same urgency I did.

I jumped on my Honda Nighthawk and took off down the road. I rode faster and faster till I realized I was going as fast as that Nighthawk could go. Although there were police officers along the route, none gave chase. I sped through Pocatello out to the jail on the southeast side of town. As I ran to the front gate, it popped open before I got to it. I ran to the next gate, same thing. Now I was at the dark windows of the central control and was motioned on. As I ran to the "E pod" door, it too popped open.

Panting with exhaustion I arrived at the control officer's desk. With a puzzled look on his face, he asked, "What are you doing here on your day off Chappy?"

I just shouted a name that came to my mind. The officer pushed the button and announced, "Chaplain Rick is here to see Rob; come to the door now!"

When the door opened, there stood Rob, eyes red from crying. Through sobs he asked, "How did you know? This is a miracle that you are here right now! In a couple more minutes, I would have shoved this into my jugular vein and taken my own life!" He held up a sharpened 20-penny nail. I took the spike from him, and out of my mouth began to pour living words of God's love, mercy, and grace. I told him of my reckless motorcycle ride into town because God told me to come. I said, "Rob, Jesus must love you big time; He just saved you from a Christ-less hell for eternity." At that Rob prayed and wept his way into the presence of Jesus, giving his heart to the Lord!

Many of my classes and services at jails were in

the evening, and I would have to ride home in the dark. Occasionally, I had some close shaves in almost hitting deer and coyotes, especially along the 25-mile stretch between American Falls and Rockland. It certainly kept us praying a lot!

Pocatello had many twisting, paved mountain roads around the hills and nearby mountains. There also was a ski hill close by that the Damascus Road Riders loved to ride during the summer months and have prayer together at the top of the mountain. Those were very special days for us as we were part of a growing, exciting ministry.

God's Amazing Provision

During this time, though, we were going through a real financial drought. Yet, as we prayed, God opened another door of income for us. Steve Isaak in American Falls raised hundreds of acres of potatoes and sugar beets. He and his family attended the Assembly of God church in American Falls. He asked if I would drive a GMC diesel 10-wheel potato/sugar beet truck to help him get in his crops. On the nights I had prison services, he would let me off early. Again, what a blessing to us!

Near the end of two months, another farmer, Brother Leisy, hired me to drive a huge 18-wheel Volvo truck. It was a challenging task as times. Hauling potatoes from the fields to the potato cellars, I had to make a 90-degree backward turn into the cellar. That was wasn't easy to do, but I made it!

When jobs were completed for the season, pastors around the district began to call us for missionary services. That was a great encouragement to us. It had been challenging to push forward in this new arena of ministry, but God was surely shining His light upon us.

As winter approached, we got a visit from Steve Kauffman from American Falls telling of God's call upon him and his wife to go on a missionary journey for a year. They wanted us to house sit for them in American Falls while they were away. They had a lovely home there, and it would put us 25 miles closer to our ministry. We thanked the Isaak's for the nine months they had let us stay in their apartment and moved into the Kauffman's home. We certainly were very comfortable there.

In the midst of all this, however, I soon faced a serious physical crisis. I contracted a serious form of the E. coli bacteria from eating venison that someone had given to us. I became deathly ill during that time, and, to make matters worse, I was allergic to the strong antibiotic needed to kill the bacteria. It took me several months to completely recover, and I was left very weak and experienced great pain in my body at times. Through God's help, I was eventually able to regain strength and the pain subsided.

Speed the Light Blessing

A wonderful blessing came our way as the Southern Idaho Youth Department raised money to purchase for us a new Speed the Light pickup truck that we needed to tow our 23-foot fifth wheel trailer. Up that that point, we had an old, high-mileage Ford pickup that was not in great condition. Our 1995 Ford 15-passenger van had some 180,000 miles on it and lacked sufficient power to pull the trailer. So, the van was given to Boise Northview church, and we were blessed to receive our new 2000 Chevy extended cab pickup!

Hells Angels

Not long afterward, I received a phone call from a CMA regional evangelist who asked me if I would accompany him to Salt Lake City, Utah, for a national motorcycle drag race. CMA had been asked to take care of security and assist in all portions of organizing the event. We also would have opportunity to minister at the event, one that was heavily sponsored by the Hells Angels motorcycle club. God was again opening a very unique door of ministry.

So, I rode my bright red Honda nighthawk to Salt Lake. The event went well. There were many world-class Harleys that could reach speeds of 200 miles per hour.

After the event, we were invited by the Hells Angels to join them for an evening dinner at a biker bar. I was not sure I wanted to go there, but after praying, I phoned Chaplain Rick Davis, who headed U.S. Missions chaplaincy ministries in Springfield. He said, "Rick you are called to a specialized ministry. You go to the lost. They won't come to you. Go with our blessing and may the Lord make you a blessing there!"

When I pulled up outside the bar, there were several Hells Angels outside directing the bikers as they parked. When they saw I was riding a red Honda, they yelled, "Get that red rice burner around the back and out of sight!" I felt very small and insignificant among these big tough guys riding their black Harleys.

Inside the bar, I felt even more like a fish out of water. But, the Hells Angels honored us and asked me to pray over the food. Several wanted to talk, and I felt God really broke down some walls that day.

After that meeting, I knew I needed to get a Harley to minister to these people and other bikers, but I didn't know how that could happen.

A Vision of God's Provision

After my return home from the biker event, Carol and I began to pack up for a return trip to the

Michigan District for another tour of ministry there.

I sold my Honda Nighthawk as I felt God was going to make a way for a Harley Davidson soon. After all, had God not provided five different airplanes and many other wonderful tools for our ministry when we needed them in the past? By faith, I believed a Harley was waiting for us in the near future, but I just didn't know how or when. We loaded up all our belongings into our fifth wheel, pickup, and Dwight's little Subaru, and took off for Michigan.

En route, we stopped at Montrose, Minnesota, to visit my oldest brother Art and his wife Marcy. The pastor at Buffalo, where my brother went to church, invited me to speak for the evening service on Sunday. As I was speaking, I had a fleeting vision of a beautiful concord-grape, full-dress Harley sitting on its kickstand right in front of the altar! I stuttered and stammered a bit but kept right on preaching.

After the service, I mentioned the peculiar vision to Art. He looked startled and said, "You saw that too?" Both of us went to the pastor and mentioned it to him who also confirmed the vision. So now, with my vision confirmed, we went forth with great anticipation of what was God going to do!

We continued to Oil City where we were invited by the Priest family to set up our fifth wheel in a trailer park they owned, complete with plug-ins and hookups. We had gotten to know the Priest's and their son Kevin when they came to Emmonak, Alaska, to do some commercial fishing. It was great to connect with them again! Their trailer park was very lush, green park with maple trees, willows, and flowers everywhere.

Vision Fulfilled

We had several missions services already set up, one of which was at Sebewaing Assembly of God. As I spoke that morning, I noticed a biker sitting in the congregation that was weeping and wiping tears all through my message. After the message, he came to me and hugged my neck, sobbing. His name was Ken Gainforth. He invited us to dinner at their home.

During dinner, Ken told us a strange story about buying a motorcycle that God told him to buy. Then, still moved to tears, he took Carol and I out to the garage and pointed to a canvas that covered an obviously large motorcycle. As he pulled off the cover, I nearly fell over. It was the exact bike I had seen in my vision in Buffalo, Minnesota—a brand new purple Harley Road Glide with all the bells and whistles! Pulling the keys from his pocket, Ken held them in front of my face and asked, "Will you ride this motorcycle for Jesus? I'll take care of everything—license, insurance, etc. Ride it to Hatfield, Arkansas, to the CMA national in two weeks and pull this trailer pod behind it with your camping gear." Carol and I had never seen such a beautiful luxurious bike in all our life. I wept all the way back home. What a miracle of provision God had again performed for us!

The Harley certainly rode differently than motorcycles I'd had before, but it was very comfortable. After we got moving, the weight of the nearly 1,000-pound bike seemed to disappear.

Ken had suggested that we ride it every day until time to leave for Hatfield so I could get used to how it handled. We even had a biker Sunday planned with Coleman Assembly of God the Sunday before we would leave for Hatfield. What a day that was! Everyone was blown away by our testimony about receiving the motorcycle.

Trip to CMA National

Immediately after the morning service, we had a picnic and then we left the church early that afternoon to get as far down the road as we could before dark on our way to Hatfield.

The next day, we were off at daybreak as we knew it was going to get very hot and humid. We rode hard, but, before long, we were cooking hot. We discovered that if we poured water on our jackets and clothing, the wind worked like an evaporative air conditioner. That really helped.

En route to Arkansas, we stopped over at John and Jan Maempa's place in Springfield, Missouri.

By this time, Carol and I were getting some serious saddle sores and feeling heat exhaustion as well. It was really great to get off the bike for a while.

John had arranged for Chaplain Rick Davis and his wife to join us for breakfast before we left for Hatfield. They were deeply blessed by the gift of the bike to us and what the Lord had done. Rick suggested that we take the back roads to Hatfield instead of the Interstate. It was less miles, but slower going as there were many stops through towns along the way; but the roadway was much more shaded and beautiful due to the forested areas we rode through.

We arrived at the Hatfield CMA headquarters around 5:00 p.m. But, we couldn't find Ken, though we knew he was there. We went ahead and put up our tent and crawled in for the night. The next morning, we discovered we were only about 100 yards from Ken's tent which was near the shower and restrooms.

This event was something entirely new to Carol and me. To see some 3,000 Christian bikers all together, worshiping and fellowshipping was awesome! It was also amazing to learn about the more than three million dollars raised annually by CMA's "Run for the Son" that went to missions endeavors and missionaries around the world. It was an amazing time.

With the CMA event completed, early Saturday

morning we took off with Ken to head back to Springfield, Missouri. We attended Central Assembly with the Maempa's, and, on Monday, we left for Michigan. The weather was so hot and humid, we could only make about 450 miles a day. It was so good to get into an air-conditioned motel room that first night; we arrived home by the second night. Surprisingly, we averaged around 43 miles per gallon with the Harley towing a 300-pound trailer. I'd owned motorcycles that wouldn't do that well with just me riding.

After arriving home, Kevin Priest and his family wanted us to house sit for them while they took a trip to Florida. So, we packed some things and went some two miles away to their home.

Deer Encounter

On the first evening after getting set up in Priest's home, we needed to pick up some milk and a few things at the store. It was hot on that July 5th, so Carol and I decided not to wear our leathers. It was only seven miles to the store after all. We did wear our helmets.

As soon as we turned onto M-20 west and accelerated to 55 miles per hour, I was looking straight into the sun. It was about 7:00 p.m., and the shadows were long on the south side. Suddenly, I saw a buck deer come bounding out of the underbrush on the south side of the road and began to cross the four lanes. Carol remembers me screaming, "Deer!" But with the sun glaring in my eyes and the deer bounding toward us, I totally misjudged the speed and slammed into the center of the deer. The bike went into a slide and then flipped violently, throwing me into the brush along the north side of the road. Carol tumbled down the road with the bike and came to a stop laying under the bike just off the pavement. I vaguely remember crying out for her as I was fading in and out of consciousness. But I didn't hear her answer. That was the lowest time in my life; I was certain she was dead. Being in shock, I couldn't move

Thankfully, someone out in their yard nearby had witnessed the accident and called 911. An officer who was watching for speeding violations just two miles away immediately responded. Also, an ambulance that was just two miles away was returning to the hospital. So, thanks to God, we had almost immediate help.

I remember someone running up to me and starting to remove my helmet. I was then placed on a gurney and loaded into the ambulance. I began crying out for Carol. The ambulance EMT said, "She is right here beside you, and even though she is badly roughed up, it's you we are keeping an eye on." Then, Carol spoke to me. That was the sweetest voice I have ever heard!

We were rushed to Midland Hospital about 15 miles east. There they immediately did preliminary exams and X-rays. Carol had a broken jaw, cracked skull, broken nose, crushed arms, and lots of abrasions. I had at least two broken ribs, a badly abrased elbow, a severely traumatized left shoulder, a numb right leg, and lots of other abrasions and bruises as well.

Once we were all bandaged up and given pain medications, we were released to go home as our bike insurance did not cover our own injuries. So, the pastor from Coleman Assembly came and got us and took us back to the Priest's home. Being full of pain meds, we slept well through the night. But the next morning was a different story! We took more pain killers and just laid around the house the first day.

Our attending physician called with the instruction, "Come in for new bandages and an exam in two days, and Carol for reconstructive surgery on her face." At this point, the reality of what had just happened to us really began to sink in. We asked the Lord, "Why? Had we become proud of the new Harley? Why this severe trial after such a miracle of provision for our ministry?" It seemed as if our dreams had suddenly been dashed upon the rocks.

Our newfound friend, Ken Gainforth, who had given us the Harley, came over and was so kind and understanding. He never questioned the Lord in this. Hobbling out to Ken's car, I directed him to the crash site. Wow! What a terrible set of skid marks and purple paint that scraped off on the road.

Broken glass, plastic, and fiberglass also were still strewn on the road. The deer was still lying off the road. With this kind of accident, there wouldn't be insurance from the other "party" to help with ambulance, hospital, and doctor bills.

Ken and I drove to the wrecking yard to look over the damage to the motorcycle. It was pretty badly damaged from tumbling down the road. There wasn't a place on the bike that wasn't crushed, broken, bent, or peeled. I was certain it would be totaled. However, a man named Phil who owned Eagle Mountain Customs motorcycle shop, had examined the bike and believed the frame had not been bent or twisted, and that he could fix it with all new factory painted parts.

Afterward, I took Carol to the reconstructive surgeon for an evaluation that we were not looking forward to. As the doctor examined her, however, he had a puzzled look on his face. "I don't understand it," he said. "Carol has just had a miracle. Every bone is in place; I don't have to touch her!" Carol and I went home rejoicing again in God's amazing love and care!

In the meantime, the insurance company gave the go-ahead on repairing the bike. So, Ken had Phil haul the Harley to his shop and they went to work on it. It took Harley Davidson some six weeks to get all the parts, but Phil did a fine job of rebuilding that miracle bike. It looked brand new! What I didn't know, however, is that Ken was working on another plan. He went back to the Harley dealer and bought *another* purple motorcycle, just like the one we had wrecked!

"Law" and "Grace"

On September 11, 2000, Ken came over to our house, and with tears streaming down his face, handed me the keys to the second brand new Harley! Carol and I stood there stunned by this completely unexpected turn of events. Ken said, "Brother Rick, God told me to do this. The repaired bike will be mine, and I will name it 'Law.' The new one will be named 'Grace.' We will ride together often and tell the story of Jesus who came to fulfill the law and bring us grace." This was all so unbelievably amazing!

I was still very sore, but able to ride. In fact, the bike seemed to strengthen my body. Four days after Ken gave us the new bike, he and I rode to Wisner, Michigan, for a huge ABATE campout and party. Due to my recent injuries, I didn't sleep well in a sleeping bag, but God certainly opened many doors of ministry through the twin purple Harleys at the event.

Carol's Amazing Resolve

Carol's first ride was on September 24, to a local ABATE chapter party and "Bike Blessing" service. God moved in awesome ways through the Bike Blessings. Most secular or outlaw bikers want to have their bikes blessed. But, we didn't just bless the bikes, we also laid our hands on the bikers and prayed over them as well. For many of the bikers, this was the first time anyone had prayed for them. They felt the touch of the Holy Spirit. Many times we got to hand out Bibles and have additional times of counseling and prayer with them.

Throughout all of this, Carol was an amazing blessing and encouragement. She didn't ride for just over two months because she was so sore, especially around her jaw which her helmet pressed against uncomfortable. Yet, I will never forget a statement she made almost immediately after the accident. She said, "Honey, I can't wait to get back on that motorcycle and punch the devil right in the face for trying to take us out!" Folks, that was the last thing I expected to hear from her right after the wreck. However, I've learned through the years that, though she may be small in stature, I also know that dynamite comes in small packages. She always has been strong willed, strong hearted, and strong in the Spirit of God, and I love her dearly for it!

We had some very warm riding clothes for the cold weather season which helped as we rode that fall to many events in chilly weather. We continued until ice and snow started covering the roads. That year, we rode right up to December. When it did snow, it warmed up enough to melt the snow soon after. So, we rode to several churches that invited us to have services during the winter. When we visited

Central Assembly of God in Muskegon, Michigan, they saw our need for a small enclosed trailer to haul our motorcycle in during bad weather and on our missionary journeys. We were so blessed! What a wonderful gift.

Increasing Acceptance

On April 25, 2001, we hooked up the trailer and loaded the Harley behind our Speed the Light pickup and took a missionary journey to Idaho for services around the Southern Idaho District. Carol and I were deeply moved by the acceptance and passion that the churches were showing to us as we pursued the new motorcycle ministry. At every church that had wide enough doors and no stairs, the pastors wanted us to ride our motorcycle into the church and park it at the altar. What an unusual yet blessed thing God was doing in our lives. What an added blessing it was to see people gather around our purple Harley at the altar, raise their hands toward heaven, and pray God's blessing over that bike and us. They prayed for God's anointing and protection and that we would be used as instruments of God's salvation, healing, and reconciliation.

Among special services we had in Idaho, I recall one we held at Central Assembly in Boise. Pastor Ted Buck had us first ride the Harley into the children's church area, in the northwest wing of the building. When that door opened, I let them hear the engine's roar and the loud pipes as we I rode in. The children were spellbound, not quite knowing what was happening. We spoke to the children and encouraged them to reach out to Jesus. From there we rode to the sanctuary entrance came down the aisle to the amazement of the congregation. Then Carol and I parked the bike at the altar and told the story of God's miraculous provision, protection, and provision again. We told of the bikers and prison inmates that were coming to Jesus with the help of this new ministry tool.

At Nampa First Assembly, Pastor Barry Osteen also had us ride the Harley into the church and park at the altar. After the service, many people wanted their picture taken on the bike, including Pastor Barry and Rebecca. Little did we know what significance that photo would have in the future.

The next day was sunny, but cold. I felt an urgency to ride to a high point overlooking the Boise valley. So, I rode to the top of Horseshoe Bend hill, praying as I rode. I felt a strange urgency in my spirit at the time and pondered in my heart what it meant.

The next Saturday, CMA had their annual "Ride for the Son" fund raiser for missionaries around the world. I rode the 100-mile ride with them as at that time Carol and I wore the CMA patch. What a powerful ministry that is. CMA raised over three million dollars worldwide for missions endeavors around the world.

Upon arriving back home to Michigan, I

participated in the annual "Baldwin Bike Blessing" on May 20. This was the largest Christian motorcycle event I have ever been involved in. There were some 40,000 bikers that showed up at the Baldwin airport from many states. A gospel music band played, and a message was delivered by a Catholic priest, followed by a time of prayer over the event.

Pastor Len Hill from the Mount Hope Church in Lansing got me involved in five different state prisons for ministry. Inmates seemed to relate to a biker and were drawn to a service where the speaker rides up in a loud, brash Harley, wearing leather covered with patches. It certainly was not the ecclesiastical attire many people are accustomed to! Somehow, however, it clicked with the culture. Many times, I saw the Lord come down and move a crowd of 30 to 90 inmates to tears with hands raised to Jesus for healing, salvation, and reconciliation. It was amazing!

On June 7, 2001, our 37th wedding anniversary, Carol and I loaded our Harley that we had named "Scarlet Grace" into the trailer and took off again for Springfield, Missouri to attend a chaplain's convention. We always loved that trip, as we also got to spend a few days with John and Jan Maempa. While in Springfield, we went on many motorcycle rides in the evening to fly our CMA colors and visit bikers wherever we could find them.

Close Call

Back in Michigan, on July 24, I rode with 13 other bikers from the Bay City CMA to Marion, North Carolina. Carol didn't go on that trip, and I was glad for her sake that she stayed behind. It was a very hot and humid ride. Additionally, we rode through pouring rain for some 1,000 miles of the 2,400-mile trip! Also, a couple riding in front of me, towing a small camp trailer, struck a raised pavement edging while changing lanes in a construction zone, and crashed hard. I nearly hit them after they went down.

I rode off the pavement into the grassy median and ran back to direct traffic until the police and ambulance arrived. All the other bikers were able to get off the road as well, which was not easy on the busy, six-lane freeway.

The biker couple were lying on the road. Thankfully, a trucker was able to pull to a stop next to them and protect them from getting hit by oncoming traffic on the blind corner. Both of them were helped off the road and were not seriously injured except for abrasions and bruises. We all followed as they were taken by ambulance to the hospital for medical assistance. The couple was able to ride the rest of the way to Marion in the chase van and trailer that accompanied our group.

Despite the challenges and mishaps on the

journey, the services at the CMA event were awesome. A number of bikers lingered at the altar till the wee hours of the morning, so hungry for more of God. Yet, on the downside, it rained every day and most of the ride back home was wet as well. Oh my, was I ever glad to get home!

Crunch!

Later, Ken Gainforth and his friend Roger left for a motorcycle trip to Daytona Beach, Florida, to minister at a biker's week there. About halfway there, they stopped at a rest area in Kentucky and parked behind a large double trailer semi. As they were opening to door to the restroom, they heard a bang and a crunching sound. Looking back, to their horror, they saw that the big rig had backed over Ken's Harley, the one we wrecked and had newly rebuilt! Then, pulling forward, the trucker ran over the bike again and took off onto the freeway.

Ken and Roger tried to get the trucker's attention, but to no avail. So, Roger got on his bike and took off after the truck. It took a while to get the trucker's attention and get him to pull over. When he did, the driver was astonished at what Roger told him, and said he hadn't heard or felt a thing when he left the rest area. But, he turned around and Ken and Roger talked with him and a police officer who collected all the information. A wrecker was called, and Ken's Harley was hauled off to Harley Davidson dealer in Radcliff, Kentucky.

After some 9 weeks, the shop called and said, "Your Harley is ready. Come and get it." Once again, the bike had been resurrected! So, Ken hopped on my Harley with me, and we rode to Radcliff. Upon arriving, sure enough, Ken's bike was like new again, with all new saddle bags, gas tank, handlebars, fenders, fairing, etc. However, the tow hitch had not been replaced on Ken's bike, so I had to tow his trailer behind mine. However, it didn't trail well. At 70 miles per hour, it would start to whip, which, on a motorcycle, isn't a good thing. It's sort of like a huge tail wagging a small dog. So, I had to keep my speed at or below 65, but we arrived home okay.

By this time, Carol and I were now deeply involved with the five prisons and three different CMA chapters in Michigan. We were very busy, and the miles on our Harley piled up quickly.

Riding Over the "Mighty Mac"

Ken, Roger, and I rode up to Gaylord, Michigan, and hooked up with a large group of "Michigan Road Riders," that numbered some 30 bikes. We rode north and crossed the famous Mackinac suspension bridge, called the "Mighty Mac." It is the fifth longest suspension bridge in the world, and quite an experience on a bike! The bridge is five miles long and rises some 200 feet above the water so that large ocean-going vessels can pass underneath. Anchorage towers rise 552 feet above the water, and the total length of the wire in the main cables is 42,000 miles! In extremely high winds or changes in weight on the bridge, the deck at the center span can move as much as 35 feet. However, most of the time movement cannot be felt. Some drivers, however, have a phobia about crossing bridges. In such cases, arrangements can be made for drivers to drive their vehicles across. Crossing the Mighty Mac was a great experience!

From there, we rode through the upper Michigan peninsula to Paradise Point. We stopped by an old lighthouse that used to guide ships around the rocky point at night and in bad weather. Today, ships are guided by GPS technology. But, the old lighthouse is kept looking like new for visitors to see. We camped at Paradise Point and rode the next day to the border of Ontario, Canada, at Sault Ste. Marie. This is also the crossing point over the channel between the United States and Canada where Lake Huron and Lake Michigan join. It was an absolutely beautiful trip. Deer, moose, bear were seen on our ride, along with amazing foliage. Most of the bikes were equipped with CB radios, and bikers asked me to share stories about flying in Alaska as we rode. It was an exceptional trip overall.

Pocatello Convention

In June 2003, CMA scheduled their National West Convention in Pocatello, Idaho at the county fairgrounds. This was amazing to us, as only eight years before, Carol and I pioneered the first CMA ride group in Pocatello. Within two years it had grown to chapter status and the Damascus Road Riders were born. Now, since our move to Michigan, the group had grown to 120 members! Now CMA would be holding a national event there. Wow!

The Bay City CMA chapter asked Carol and me if we would escort them on the trip to Pocatello. We were glad to do so, but the day before leaving, our Harley developed an engine noise that would require tearing the engine down. So, we decided to drive our Speed the Light pickup with our bike trailer and be the chase vehicle in case a bike broke down on the trip. Ken and Roger were going to come a couple of days later, so they wouldn't be riding with us.

The trip went well until we hit the mountains. One of the riders that had an older motorcycle had difficulty towing his heavy pop-up trailer. Riding up the mountain road against head winds caused his engine to overheat. So, we loaded his pop-up trailer into our trailer and went on.

Just as we were crossing the high country at about the 7,000-foot level out of Laramie, Wyoming, we ran into a bad storm. Large hail, some three-quarters of an inch in diameter, pelted the riders, raising some welts and breaking the headlight on one of the bikes. We stopped as soon as we could and got everyone under cover until the storm passed. From there we got to a motel in Rock Springs, Wyoming, and soaked in hot tubs and rubbed sore muscles.

The next day, we traveled on to Pocatello, arriving in the early afternoon. We all registered for the CMA event and got our camp spots reserved. We set up our tents and enjoyed our first evening service under the huge roof of the fair bleachers. When Ken and Roger arrived the next day, they set up their camp next to ours.

We sat around and talked about the beginnings of CMA in this region and had a meal before the evening service. And what a service! God was surely using CMA to further the gospel to people that most could never reach. As Carol and I watched, the sun set around the mountains on which we had taken many rides and prayed for revival over this very area. Now we were amazed at what God had wrought!

The next day was a free day until the evening service, so many of the bikers asked me to lead them on a tour to the mountains, a ski hill, Mink Creek camp, and other beautiful areas. So, Ken told me to ride his bike, the one he had first given us, and lead the group with it. I was so full of praise and worship unto the Lord on that ride. At times it was hard to see for the tears of joy that flowed freely as I remembered the birth of this ministry here. We climbed the twisting road to Mink Creek forest camp ground and ate the lunches we had brought with us. As the creek nearby gurgled down the mountain, my tears just kept coming. I was overjoyed.

The tour came off with no bikers down. Praise the Lord! When we got back to our camp, CMA leader Mike Bachman came over to see me at our tent. He knew we were planning to move back to Idaho in September, and he asked me to be a chaplain at the maximum-security prison. Again, tears overwhelmed me, as I realized that God was again going before us to pave the way. After the convention, we parted our ways and traveled back to Michigan, thankfully, without any problems.

Return to Idaho

As Carol and I began to look West again realizing we would soon be going back to Idaho, we pondered in our hearts the direction our ministry would take. We felt God would be moving us to pioneer another biker ministry along with prison ministry when we got back to Idaho. But, I also felt uneasy about how we would start another CMA chapter in the Treasure Valley.

Carol and I had been wearing the CMA patch for nine years and had attended at least six national CMA events. We also had ministered at numerous state and local events. We loved CMA and the ministries it represented.

CMA had a chapter in Boise called "R Wheels R His." Carol and I had ridden with them several times in Run for the Son fund raisers and other events. They were doing a fine job. But, I felt we needed another chapter in the Nampa, Kuna, Caldwell region, centering it in Nampa.

I received a phone call from my sister Appy Mae Gillatt in Nampa. She wanted to sell her property and home and build a smaller house in the Middle Creek Drive subdivision. After we talked, it seemed as if God was opening doors for us to purchase her home. We all went to prayer about that, and as the deal materialized, we signed the papers for the purchase.

Carol and I had begun riding with "Soul Zone Motorcycle Riders" out of the large Mount Hope Church in Lansing, Michigan. When they realized we were moving back to Idaho, we talked about possibly taking Soul Zone to Idaho and change the patch to the State of Idaho instead of Michigan. We took their information and kept the idea in the back of our minds. However, I still wanted to pioneer a CMA chapter if at all possible as they already had established a good reputation in the biker world.

It seemed that God was calling us again to be fire starters. I rode several more times to the five prisons and the three retirement centers where Carol and I had been ministering. They certainly did not want us to go, and Carol and I were very torn by the prospect of leaving as well. I understood how the Apostle Paul must have felt when it was time to leave the churches in Asia that he had established to go on another missionary journey.

Shortly after completing final services with churches around the Michigan District, I received a call from Barry Osteen, pastor of Nampa First Assembly of God. He asked if we would consider becoming resident missionaries in their church and start a motorcycle ministry. Wow! Was God putting this together or what? Again, details were being laid out even before we left. We advertised our 14- by 70-foot house trailer and soon sold it for the asking price! We had a large yard sale and sold everything that we couldn't fit into our 6- by 10-foot covered trailer and our extended cab pickup.

On August 19, 2003, we headed for Idaho. Dwight drove our pickup and Carol rode with him. I rode our purple Harley, towing the pod trailer loaded to the hilt.

The trip went well with few problems. The Harley lost the electronic cruise control and turn signal caused by the transmission speed sensor shorting out. So, I had to use hand signals the rest of the trip. We averaged some 500 miles a day, stayed in motels, and ate at fast-food places along the way.

As we got into Idaho, some 250 miles southeast of Boise, the weather became very hot, rising to 100 degrees, then to 105; and as we crossed through a desert area by Mountain Home, the thermometer read 110! I was baking on the Harley. I drank quarts of water and other fluids and poured water over my clothes to provide evaporative air conditioning. It was miserable!

Then, as we neared Boise, we spotted ominous black clouds moving toward us. I stopped to put on my rain gear. Shortly after, we were hit by 40- to 50-mile-per-hour winds and torrential rain. We kept on going, though we shouldn't have, as the wind and water nearly swept me off the road. But we were so close to the finish line we just wanted to get home. Finally, at 4:30 in the afternoon, we arrived at our newly purchased home. Debris from the passing storm was everywhere, but, thankfully, our property was spared major damage.

There had been a construction delay in completing my sister's new home, so she was not moved out when we arrived. All her belongings were in numerous boxes in the house. We navigated on trails around the boxes; even the garage was full. So, we just left most of our belongings in the trailer, taking out only essential items. We camped with Appy Mae for about three weeks till her home was finished and inspected. Believe it or not, it was fun! In the meantime, I had completed tests and training with the Idaho Department of Corrections (IDOC) for ministering in the maximum-security area of the prison.

One day, I took a solo ride to the top of Bogus Basin, a well-known ski mountain outside of Boise, and found a clear spot where I could look over the entire Treasure Valley. I could see Mountain Home to the east and Ontario, Oregon, to the west. As it was getting dark, I began to pray on the purple

Harley. The Holy Spirit really began to move on me as I looked upon the darkening valley with sunlight still on the mountaintop. The scarlet thread of paint over the Harley's purple background reminded me of the death and resurrection of Jesus Christ and the torn veil in the Temple at Jerusalem. As lights began coming on in the valley, I saw this as the light of the gospel of Jesus that would shine into the lives of many people in the days, weeks, months, and years to come.

How wonderful it is when the Lord gives us a clear vision of what He wants us to do! Proverbs 29:18 begins with, "Where there is no vision, the people perish." The term *vision* in the Hebrew language means "revelation." When we do not obey the revelation of the Lord, then it is easy for God's people to lose biblical convictions and cast aside moral restraints which eventually leads to spiritual death. I knew in my heart that our new motorcycle ministry would need to be built on prayer and the unadulterated Word of God.

It was a beautiful trip down the mountain seeing the ever-increasing glow of lights in the valley as I descended. What a revelation from the Lord!

Motorcycle Invasion

Carol and I began working side by side with the R Wheels R His CMA chapter. Together we did a motorcycle prison "invasion" at the farm prison south of Boise. There must have been some 30 motorcycles and 50 riders that rode inside the prison walls that day. We staged a motorcycle show with all our shiny bikes lined up for the inmates to see and to talk with us. An officer with a camera took photos of the inmates with us by our bikes. Afterward, a great gospel band and singing group ministered. Then several of the ministry team previously had been inmates in this very prison gave their testimonies of what the Lord had done in their lives, proclaiming hope to the hopeless!

Mike Bachman preached the Word while we moved around through hundreds of inmates, inviting them to come to Jesus. When the altar call was given, some 37 inmates came forward for salvation. Eight of them were baptized in a portable tank that had been set up. Praise the Lord!

"Soul Zone Idaho" Is Born

I began to share with the tri-state CMA coordinator about possibly starting another CMA chapter in the Treasure Valley. He felt like it would be better for the time being to just build on already established chapters. After much more prayer, I shared with Pastor Osteen about my vision on the mountain a few weeks earlier. Then he asked me if I would consider pioneering "Soul Zone Motorcycle Riders" out of Nampa First Assembly. I went home and shared this with Carol. We prayed and gave it to Jesus. Soon we went to Pastor Barry and said, "We will do it!" So, Soul Zone Motorcycle Riders of Idaho was born. We dearly loved CMA, and desired God's blessing upon them. My vision was that we could minister side by side with all the Christian biker groups in the valley.

At first, there were only five or six bikers that rode with us under Soul Zone, but soon riders from other groups and churches became interested. In fact, several riders from First Church of the Nazarene began riding with us as they had no Christian ride group in their church, and they asked to become patch-wearing members. Also, people from "Bikers for Christ" and "Christian Crusaders" began riding with us. Soon, there were several men from our church that got excited about riding and the potential ministry that could come out of it. They bought motorcycles and started riding. Even Pastor Barry and Rebecca bought a motorcycle and joined with us.

One concern was that some riders were not used to riding motorcycles, which resulted in two minor accidents in the group almost immediately. So, some took a motorcycle riding safety course that really helped in their ability to ride and understand motorcycle safety.

As more became involved, we drafted an initial constitution and bylaws for membership and began having regular monthly meetings. Soon afterward, a group called "Reborn Motorcycle Riders" from Mountain Home began to attend our meetings and ride with us whenever they could.

Prison Invasion Partnership

In partnership with CMA, we began to plan the next Prison Motorcycle Invasion at the farm prison. This would be Soul Zone's first big outreach. After everyone had received their security clearances, on May 22, 2004, we all rode to the Lowe's store parking lot in Boise and met up with the CMA leader Mike Bachman and his group. Following further instructions about prison ministry and a time of prayer, some 25 motorcycles, many of them with two people on board, headed to the prison. After security clearance, the prison gate opened, and we all revved our engines. Many had really loud pipes. What a racket! Some 700 inmates were in the yard, all smiling and waving as we rode into the prison yard.

Several guards were positioned around the gate as we rode around a paved turnaround and lined up and parked the bikes. Each of us stayed by our bikes as the inmates came over to talk with us. Many again had photos taken with us by a security officer.

Soon afterward, the music began from the CMA singers and band. They sang and played beautifully, and former inmates gave their testimonies of what Jesus had done in their lives. Mike Bachman preached the Word while others of us connected with inmates doing one-to-one ministry with them and inviting them to come to Jesus. What a powerful time as we witnessed the tears of many inmates as they came to Jesus! This time, 51 inmates came forward for salvation and we baptized 12 in water. What a powerful time we had!

Not long after this, the group from the Nazarene church came to our monthly meeting and noted that the national office of the Church of the Nazarene had just adopted their own motorcycle group called the "Road Riders for Jesus." They asked if we would be offended it they replaced their Soul Zone patches with their new name. They assured us that they wanted to continue working together with us for the kingdom of God. We gave a hundred percent approval for what they were doing and soon Road Riders for Jesus was born.

Ministering in Maximum Security

By this time, I was riding to the maximum-security prison two to three times weekly for services, teaching the course, *Man in the Mirror,* with up to 10 inmates at a time. At other times, there would be nearly 40 inmates out of their cells in a large room with steel tables and stools bolted to the concrete floor, sitting around, reading, playing cards, watching TV, walking laps, doing pushups, or talking on phones. I would simply sit there and talk with them, discussing Scriptures and praying with them. It could get crazy in there at times. Occasionally there would be fights, sometimes very violent ones, calling for code blue officer intervention. Instigators would sometimes be shackled in chains and escorted to the "hole," a tiny solitary room with a hard bunk and only Nutribread to eat.

Amazingly, I visited men in the hole who came to Jesus there. Sometimes experiencing solitary caused some to realize they were out of control and needed help and a Savior.

It was a joy to have many services around the Southern Idaho District and visit many churches as well. They always seemed to feel our heartbeat for the lost souls and support us with their prayers and finances.

"Mini-Sturgis"

On September 26, 2004, we had a "Mini-Sturgis" motorcycle invasion at the Autumn Winds assisted living center in Caldwell with Bikers for Christ. What fun this was! The workers there had apprised the elderly residents of our coming. When our group of loud motorcycles rolled in, the residents were all outside laughing and waving. Some hugged our necks after we rode up and parked. One old grandma in a wheelchair wheeled up to me and asked, "Can I twist that throttle? I've never gotten to do that before." So, I let her grab the throttle and she twisted it wide open and the loud pipes really crackled! I wondered if she was going to blow up my engine as she laughed with glee! One former Hells Angels rider who had come to Jesus dearly loved it when we came for services.

Biker Sunday Gang War

On October 10, 2004, we had our first Soul Zone Motorcycle Riders of Idaho Biker Sunday. It was cool, but fairly nice weather. Thirty riders had signed up for the bike show and bike games. During the service, the Lord's presence was so precious as we worshiped and sang together. I preached my first Biker Sunday sermon.

After the message and prayer, we all moved into the dining room for chili and cornbread; then we went outside for the bike show and games. Not long after we had gone outside, the completely unexpected happened as, suddenly, two rival gangs got into a shootout close to the church! Loud rapid-fire gunshots rang out. A bullet blew out the rear tire of the motorcycle parked next to mine! Everyone in the parking lot ducked down or hit the pavement as the bullets zinged all around us. We were caught in their crossfire! Bricks broke and sprayed red dust as the bullets hit the side of the church. Gang members swinging baseball bats ran down the street chasing each other.

After dialing 911, the police came, but by then, the gangs had taken off. After realizing no one had been injured, with one voice, we gave praise and thanks, to the Lord for His protection! Sadly, the gangs chased each other to Caldwell and, in another shootout later that same night, some deaths occurred.

Ongoing Ministry Outreaches and Events

As winter approached, the rest of the year was hit and miss as far as riding motorcycle was concerned. If the roads were snow or ice covered, we drove four-wheelers with the heater and wipers on. But if the roads were clear and the sun was shining, I put on my cold weather gear and rode. I rode mostly to the prison and motorcycle events during the winter months. But, in the spring of 2005, on April 2, we had our first "Jericho Run." We joined with Bikers for Christ and CMA who provided their big tent for the chili and other foods. This would be a unique prayer ride and a "Scrabble Run" for a prize. The run was 55 miles long around Canyon County, ending up at Lakeview Park in Nampa for the rally. Live music, chili, and a bike show were scheduled. Some 149 motorcycles showed up for the event. We served 250 meals and raised $2,200 for the local police department's chaplaincy program in the Nampa/Caldwell area.

On April 11, we took our purple Harley to Twin Falls for District Council. We set up a colorful missions display there with our bike and played a DVD video of a Jericho Run and other biker events around the state. Throughout that summer, we scheduled many other rides that included ministry and humanitarian outreaches of various kinds. Soul Zone continued to grow and expand their ministries. It was no longer only about riding motorcycles together. Members got involved with a variety of different ministries including the following:

- **Friday night ride**, usually a weekly, 50-plus mile tour to various places of interest with a stop somewhere to eat and have prayer and fellowship.
- **Busted Shovel Bar & Grill church services** in Meridian, pastored by a Soul Zone member, Jim Atkins. Attendance has been around 70 to 90 people, and many people have been baptized.
- **Retirement center** services around the valley.
- **Prison ministry.** Various members are certified to enter the state prison system for church services, one-to-one ministry, and classes. Prison invasions are done in partnership with CMA and other Christian biker groups.
- **Syringa House ministry** where members have ongoing Bible study and special events for troubled young women.
- **Pie runs** on Thanksgiving Day for all police and emergency service units around the Nampa area. Some 50 pies are delivered along with a time of prayer and fellowship.
- **Hope House** fund raiser for homeless children.
- **Hospital visits** for the sick and injured, offering prayer and personal ministry.
- **Single Moms** ministry night.

Additionally, Soul Zone members have been

involved with "God and Country" Christian festivals and fireworks on July 4, bike shows around the valley, and have served as honor guards for military funerals and other special events.

Return to Michigan

By the spring of 2007, Carol and I felt an urgency to return to Michigan to help shore up the prison ministry that we left when we moved to Idaho in 2003. So, after communicating with the Chaplaincy Department about it, Carol and I handed the Soul Zone Motorcycle Riders of Idaho to Nampa First Assembly to expand the ministry and take it to another level, which they certainly did. Before we left, Pastor Barry Osteen commented that Soul Zone had become the most successful outreach ministry of the church.

As we prepared to travel to Michigan, I remembered again the last service I had led at Riverside State Prison in Ionia in August 2003. There must have been 90 inmates in that service. The Holy Spirit fell on those inmates that day. After I preached the Word and called for salvation response, I told them that this was our last service with them. They began to weep as I prayed the closing prayer.

By prison rules, the inmates are supposed to line up and leave the chapel and go back to their cells. But, instead, they lined up and, one by one, hugged my neck and wept. I kindly reminded them that they were supposed to go to their cells, yet the officers only smiled and allowed all the inmates to say goodbye in this manner. Then most of them waited for me outside the chapel and walked with me as far as the inner gate of the prison yard.

I was in tears as I walked out the last gate and to my motorcycle. As I was putting on my helmet, I heard loud voices chanting, "Please, Chaplain Rick, come back. We need you and love you!" I could still hear those words ringing in my ears 10 years later.

Nampa First Assembly bought our smaller single axle 6- by 10-foot trailer for Youth Department trips. We then purchased a new 7- by 14-foot tandem-axle trailer for our trip back to Michigan. On our way, we stopped to attend the Southern Idaho District Council in Twin Falls, Idaho. After that, we left to attend the Wyoming District Council, then went on to my brother Art and Marcy's home in Montrose, Minnesota.

We were loaded very heavily with all our earthly belongings, including two motorcycles. We averaged only nine miles per gallon. On Sunday in Montrose, I spoke during the Sunday School hour, and Art and I sang and played our guitars during the service. The sweet Holy Spirit was there to bless souls. After leaving Montrose, Art had two more heart attacks calling for seven stints in his heart and he also battled cancer. Marcy had serious neck surgery to fuse some broken bones in her spine.

Though they were aging, their spirits and love for the Lord did not waver.

We arrived at the place we were going to stay for the next year to 18 months and set up housekeeping. Again, Kevin Priest provided a great place for us to stay at a very low cost to us. There was a two-car garage attached, so we had plenty of room for our Speed the Light Ford Expedition and two motorcycles.

When I went to check out the status of prison ministry with Len Hill at Mount Hope Church, I found that Riverside Prison had been closed, and the inmates that were there were sent to other prisons. However, we could not find out where they went. I cried out to God for an answer on where to start. Then Len suggested he could really use my help at the St. Louis facility which was only 12 miles from our home instead of 80-plus miles otherwise. I gladly agreed to do so.

Wonderful Reunion

After my state exam and orientation meeting, I was assigned to teach the *12 Steps to Wholeness* course for 16 inmates who had enrolled. Going out for my first class, I nearly fell on my face, when, opening the door, inmates cried out, "Chaplain Rick, you came back!" It was the same guys from Riverside Prison who had called out to me when I left 10 years before! Wow! I immediately knew we were going to have a great class, and we surely did!

God had so wonderfully intervened again.

I was so blessed one day as I was leaving the prison. When about halfway across the yard, the deputy warden was walking to another cell block and saw me across the yard. He came quickly over to me and hugged me saying, "Thank you, Chaplain Rick, you make our work easier. After you leave, the inmates you have taught go out and be salt and light to the rest of the inmates, bringing peace to this place."

Motorcycle Ministry Expanded

Shortly after this visit, the pastor of Oil City Assembly of God asked me, "Would you begin an Assemblies of God Honorbound Motorcycle Riders group in our church?" I agreed to do so. So, we began to visit other Christian and secular motorcycle groups around the area and join them on their rides and tours. The Honorbound motorcycle patch was a very large and beautiful one, and it attracted a lot of attention. Soon, we had six to 12 motorcycles and some of them with two riders. We met at the church in Oil City on Friday evenings at 6:30 and had prayer together. Then we rode some 25-50 miles around the area and stopped somewhere for dinner and fellowship.

Though the members were having a great time and knew that we would be returning back to Idaho soon, there didn't seem to be anyone interested in taking on the leadership of this group. Without strong leadership and a call of God to make a difference in peoples' lives, the group would not survive. Thankfully, however, there was a strong CMA group in Mount Pleasant only seven miles away and other Christian groups involved in biker ministry. The Michigan District already had one biker church and was planning on another one soon. Many of the Assemblies of God churches in the district had strong biker ministries or were deeply involved with CMA and other groups.

Overall, Carol and I really felt that things were moving forward and that our mission work in Michigan was coming to an end. We had missionary services in some 28 churches during our 18 months there. I also was the speaker at the district's Royal Rangers pow-wow at Lost Lake campground. I rode my Harley to the pulpit at the start of every service. The boys loved it. Many of them gave their hearts to Jesus during those days and were filled with the Holy Spirit.

Back to Idaho

Since we had sold our home in Idaho, we needed to have a place available when we left Michigan. I received a call from a good friend that had a three-bedroom house for rent. Again, it seemed that the Lord had closed one door and opened another. Soul Zone Motorcycle Riders of Idaho sent us a letter of invitation to return to that ministry. With the present biker culture, we knew we would not be able to bring Honorbound Motorcycle ministries to Idaho, at least not at this time.

In late August 2008, we packed for our trip back to Idaho. We deeply loved our ministry in Michigan. We were privileged to touch so many people from different walks of life. We also loved the beauty of the area. Mount Pleasant was well named as it was a nice green lush area that received much more rain than we do in Idaho. In fact, many of the farmers rarely irrigated as it usually rained enough for their crops to grow. Most roadways were line with beautiful woods and foliage.

Our trip back to Idaho went well. No flats or mechanical problems; we just burned a lot of gas. Our tandem-axle trailer again was packed with our motorcycles and all the earthly goods we could cram in around them. It was heavy! Our Ford Expedition pulled it well, but with 20 to 30 mile-per-hour headwinds oftentimes, our mileage dropped to seven to nine miles per gallon.

Just before leaving for Idaho, we had learned that my sister Appy Mae had cancer. Upon arriving home, Carol and I asked to go with my sister to the doctor for a report on the status of her cancer and prognosis. Appy Mae's daughter Linda and husband Ted Buck, pastor of Boise Central Assembly, and other family members also met with us. We were stunned by the prognosis. Appy Mae was terminal with only two to three weeks to live. Sadly, true to the prognosis, she passed into the Lord's presence within two weeks. Though we had earnestly prayed for her healing, clearly it was time for her to go home. She was now with her Lord and husband Reginald who had passed some 10 years before. They had both served in pastoral ministry for many years.

The family put her house up for sale after her passing; however, the housing market in 2008 was very poor. So, in September 2009, Pastor Ted and Linda, who had assumed responsibility for the house, called Carol and me and asked, "Would you consider moving into Appy Mae's home and just pay us a small rent?" We were in shock and overjoyed at the idea. So, with great joy, we began the move. Her house was only a mile from where we lived, so, with our trailer and help from Soul Zone members, we moved very quickly. What a lovely home with so much room and an insulated garage. We were so blessed!

Almost immediately, we began hosting our church's home group meetings and experienced awesome moves of God in those times. We began to see souls being saved around our table. We also became deeply involved in Soul Zone again which now had some nine different ministries underway.

Health Crisis

Some three years later, Carol and I faced a crisis we would have never expected. On a Saturday evening in February 2012, during a men's retreat in Cascade, I received an urgent call from Carol.

"Honey, please come home immediately!" she said. "My jaw is swelling terribly and the pain is excruciating!"

I immediately grabbed my bags and left for home around 9 p.m. It was near midnight when I arrived home to Carol crying out in pain with a visibly swollen jaw. It seemed she had a badly infected molar. But, what could I do late on a Saturday night? I frantically searched the phone book and Internet for a local dentist that could see her on a Sunday morning. I did find one, and Carol and I went to his office early that morning. The dentist determined that Carol did have an infected molar and it would have to be pulled. She also would have to take antibiotics to fight severe infection.

"Carol is allergic to most antibiotics," I told the doctor. He assured me that the antibiotic was gentle.

We used the antibiotic, but, as we feared, Carol had a severe reaction and ended up in the emergency room. Not only did she have a bad reaction, her infection spread. So, another antibiotic was administered which resulted in uncontrollable bloody diarrhea which turned into Clostridium difficile infection, or "C diff," as it's generally referred to. Being a very serious and contagious condition, Carol was put in quarantine.

Since there appeared to be no antibiotic that Carol could tolerate, she went downhill rapidly, losing much weight and growing weaker by the day. Much prayer went up for Carol during this very trying time. Eventually, her doctor said, "I am sorry, but there is nothing more medically that can be done." He signed documents to place Carol in hospice care.

Afterward, the doctor who signed the hospice document conferred with a pharmacist who suggested using a new and experimental medication. This involved drinking several small doses of the medication mixed with a flavoring to make it more palatable. It had worked for some patients experiencing similar symptoms to Carol's. So, we tried it, and it did kill the C diff; however, she had been sick with the infection too long. The damage done to her digestive system was medically irreversible.

Carol was now down to 82 pounds and unable to eat much at all. Hospice was scheduled to come around noon one July day to discuss arrangements for taking Carol to the nursing home. I feared this would possibly be her last ride. She cried almost constantly with pain. Only strong opioids could help lessen her suffering.

During this time, my only consolation was Philippians 4:13, "I can do all things through Christ which strengthens me." I spent hours laying on the floor crying out to God for strength. I too lost over 30 pounds just from the stress, sleeplessness, and not eating well.

In a very weak voice, I heard Carol call for me. I

immediately went to her, and she put out her thin, weak arms and said, "Honey, please take me in your arms."

I knelt over her and took her frail body into my arms, and she gripped me tightly, saying, "Honey, now please pray that Jesus will just take me home now. I cannot suffer anymore, if Jesus is not going to heal me."

I began to pray, cuddling her frail body. But, how could I do this? What could I say? I loved her so much. I prayed, "Dear Jesus, You know how much I love the wife you gave me. How faithful we have been to each other! But, Jesus, if you are going to take her home, I now lay her in Your arms to take her to her reward. If I must finish our task on earth alone, I accept that responsibility now."

Shortly after, there was a knock at the door. It was Heart & Home Hospice. Three ladies had arrived to take Carol to the nursing home. But, remarkably, they said, "God told us all to anoint Carol with oil of healing and pray before we take her." Wow! This was not expected, but God's presence was powerful! In fact, Carol was smiling after the prayer.

Miraculous Recovery

We all left to take Carol to the nursing home. After getting back home, I was so exhausted that I slept for 12 hours straight. I hadn't slept well in weeks. As soon as I got up, it was nearing noon, so I went quickly to the nursing home to see Carol. When I went into her room, she was standing by her bed with the biggest smile on her face! She said, "Honey, I feel so much better and I am so hungry! Please walk me to the lunch room to eat lunch!" She hadn't been hungry in weeks.

Carol ate the whole plate of food, and did so the rest of the week. Gaining strength and health daily, the nursing home told us, "You just take her home. She doesn't need to be here anymore."

After taking Carol home, right away, she was singing, eating well, working in the house and garden and gaining weight. Though kept on a medication for emotional stability, her physical health returned. Praise God! Carol has been able to go with me to prison to minister to the inmates, and they just love her. She rides to motorcycle events with me and ministers in the Autumn Winds retirement center and has become chaplain for Soul Zone Motorcycle Riders!

Ministry Growth and Challenges

In the time that has followed, Soul Zone has continued to grow in number and in ministries. Dan Tietsort became president in 2006 and led Soul Zone into some new, uncharted areas. However, during Carol's serious illness, Dan experienced a devastating and debilitating stroke that left him paralyzed on the left side, nearly blind, and in a wheelchair. Soul Zone has deeply loved him and his wife Loretta as they have been such a loving, serving part of us all. Soul Zone Motorcycle Riders voted unanimously to make them lifetime honorary members of our group. They still make it to many events, and though they are in the midst of a storm, they are still an awesome part of Soul Zone's ministries.

There are many things in life that are hard to understand. Truly, God's ways are not our ways. But His ways are always the right ways. Though I do not understand the reasons we must experience trials, nor do I know what the future holds, with the Apostle Paul, I can declare, *"For I know whom I have believed, and am persuaded that he is able to keep that which I have committed unto him against that day"* (2 Timothy 1:12, KJV). As an old song says, "Life trials will seem so small when we see Christ." It further declares, "One glimpse of His dear face, all sorrows will erase." What a marvelous hope we have!

New Home

In May 2017, Carol, Dwight, and I opened another new chapter in our lives as we moved to a new home in Caldwell. Our family found it necessary to sell Appy Mae's house in which we had lived for nine years in Nampa. In view of that, we felt it wise to purchase a smaller home in the area and prepare for possible retirement in the future. As Carol and I are now in our 70's, and our son Dwight is in very poor health, we see the sunset of this life coming rapidly.

We looked at several older homes that were for sale, but each of them seemed priced too highly for their condition; all needed much repair and upgrading. A realtor friend, Lynn Moore, told us about a new 1,300-square foot Hubble home that was nearing completion in Caldwell. We went to see it and loved what we saw. After some prayer and negotiating, we closed the deal on our new home.

The next three weeks or so were abuzz with packing boxes, hauling junk to the dump, yard sales, etc. We still had our large trailer and our Ford Expedition to haul our possessions the five miles to our new home. On May 22, some husky men helped us move appliances, furniture, a heavy tool chest, and more. Once inside, we unpacked, hung curtains, installed blinds, etc. Then on July 1, we had a house warming party.

Most of the homes had established front lawns and a sprinkler system, but no shrubbery, trees, or flowers. So, we had a landscaper come who did a great job on the backyard. We also put an 8- by 8-foot shed in the back for lawn equipment and stuff we don't use all the time. We are thankful for our lovely new home for as long as the Lord allows us.

Our black Speed the Light Ford Expedition had served us well since 2006 and now logged some

262,000 miles. It needed significant repair, which didn't seem advisable, so, in August, Speed the Light gave us permission to sell it and send them the money, which we did. We bought a 2014 Chevy Spark, a cute little car that's fun to drive and averages some 38 miles per gallon.

With no way to pull our utility trailer, so we sold it too. We have also bid farewell to our Harley that had carried us to countless ministry events and outreaches and holds so many memories. I just couldn't handle its 950 pounds anymore. Thankfully, it was purchased by a Pentecostal pastor, so it is still in the ministry! In its place, we now have a Suzuki 650 Boulevard, with a large windshield, saddlebags, and a comfortable back rest for Carol. It is much lighter and easier to handle, though maybe not as comfortable to ride as the Harley.

Looking Back as We Go Forward

Carol and I not only had the privilege of founding the Soul Zone Motorcycle Riders ministry in Idaho, but we also now serve as president and chaplain. We go weekly to the Idaho State Correctional Center, Idaho's largest prison, to preach and teach Jesus to the inmates, something we have done for 25 years since leaving Alaska in 1992. Pastor Ray Rhoads, who has been with Soul Zone from the beginning, goes with me every second week for services at the prison. He also assists with weddings and visitation within the biker community.

Additionally, we minister together at the Autumn Winds retirement center three times a month. Some of the residents are retired bikers. We ride regularly from April through October and are deeply involved with many ministries throughout the year.

As we look back over the years, we are amazed and humbled by the awesome privilege to serve the Kingdom of God in so many ways. While there have been many challenges, some difficult to understand, we have always been keenly aware of God's hand guiding, anointing, protecting, and providing—ordering our steps day by day. To Him belongs all the glory, honor, and praise!

While this may be the final chapter in "Unto the End of the Earth," it will not be the last story of our lives and ministry. Carol and I hope and pray that all who read this book will be challenged to do more, to be all they can be for Jesus, to be challenged to new and seemingly impossible exploits for the Kingdom of God, till Jesus comes to take us all to His reward.

May you feel the call as we have felt the call of God on our lives. As the Apostle Paul declared in Philippians 4:13, *"I can do all things through Christ which strengtheneth me"* (KJV).

May you follow the command of our Lord Jesus Christ, *"Go ye therefore, and teach all nations, baptizing them in the name of the Father, and of the Son, and of the Holy Ghost: Teaching them to observe all things whatsoever I have commanded you: and, lo, I am with you always, even* **unto the end of the world**" (Matthew 28:19, 20, KJV, emphasis added). Amen!